POW-83

"The powerful true story of what really happened to American Prisoners of War in the Japanese Death Camps in the Philippines during World War II and of one man's struggle to survive at the hands of his brutal captors."

By John W. Wallace

The Gray Rider Publishing Company
Chatham, New York
November, 1999

The Gray Rider Publishing Company
143 Longview Drive
Chatham, N.Y. 12037
Tel/Fax: (518) 392-7062

First Edition

Library of Congress Catalog Card Number: 99-65073

ISBN 0-9673733-0-1

Cover Art by Julie Brown, Canaan, NY
Edited by Steven Orr, Delmar, NY

Printed in the United States of America

ACKNOWLEDGEMENTS

To Debbie Allen, a good friend and owner of Black Dome Press, in Hensonville, NY. Thank you for your honest, professional advise and technical assistance, which helped me move this book from my computer to the printing press.

To Joe C. at the Greenpoint, Brooklyn, New York neighborhood Website located at: www.greenpointusa.com. Thank you for providing a site containing valuable historical and neighborhood information about Greenpoint and to the visitors to his site who emailed me with additional neighborhood information.

To my sister Jean Wallace. Thank you for taking the time out of your busy schedule to format the book correctly and get it ready for the printer.

To my wife Stacy and to my daughters Allison, Kathleen and Mary. Thank you for your unwavering support and love.

CONTENTS

FOREWORD

I never thought that I would ever write a book, never mind a book about a man who was held by the Japanese as a prisoner of war in World War II. Almost everyone, at one time or another, thinks about what it would be like to be in another person's shoes, to live their lives, even for just a few days. It's not hard to imagine what it would be like to be a movie star, rock singer, famous athlete, successful politician or some other well-known celebrity, with other people idolizing you and catering to your every need.

When I lived in New York City, I used to ride the subway almost every day. During those long and sometimes boring rides, I would pass the time by looking at the other people on the subway car and wondering what was going on in their lives. I wondered what kind of work they did, whether they were rich or poor, single or married. What were their lives like?

I have always been an inquisitive person, and that is probably why I joined the New York State Police in 1966. In the ensuing years, I was promoted and transferred several times. In 1992, after being transferred to headquarters in Albany, my family and I settled in the small town of Chatham, in beautiful Columbia County, New York.

As part of our normal family practice, we continued to attend mass every Sunday, but now it was in a smaller parish, Saint James, in the Village of Chatham. As we began attending mass at Saint James, I noticed that

7

there was a car parked in front of the church before and after the 8:30 AM mass, with a New York license plate that read: POW-83. It was quite a while before I managed to see who the driver was. He was an older man, about seventy-five years old at the time, who I recognized as the regular usher at the mass. He seemed to be there, without fail, every Sunday. I never approached him to ask him any questions, although I was curious about the circumstances under which he had become a prisoner of war.

What horrible things this man must have experienced as a prisoner of war, I thought. What horrible things all prisoners of war must experience! Here was a man who seemed no different from any other man his age. He came early to mass every Sunday, helped out by ushering, and then went home right after mass. He never seemed to hang around to talk with other parishioners. He didn't go to the Chatham Bakery or the Whitestone Restaurant after mass for breakfast or a cup of coffee as is the common practice of many parishioners, including my wife, Stacy, and myself. Other than nodding a quick hello to those he knew, or asking them to assist him in taking up the collection, he pretty much kept to himself.

One Sunday in the spring of 1993, he came over to where I was sitting with my family and asked me if I wouldn't mind helping him out. We exchanged some small talk, and I found out his name was John Mackowski and he had been born and raised in the Greenpoint section of Brooklyn. It did not take long before I became a "regular" usher at the 8:30 mass with John Mackowski and a few others: Dan Flynn, Pat Clifford, Bill Scanell, Stan Novine and Tracy Crandall. It also wasn't long before my curiosity got the best of me and I called upon my interviewing skills, developed as an investigator, to gingerly ask John about his past.

Over the next several years, with a great deal of prodding on my part, John eventually opened up. He told me about his experiences as a young man growing up in Brooklyn and the circumstances under which he became a prisoner of war. He was able to recall these experiences very clearly. Even after so many years, he still knew the names and nicknames of those he served with in the military. After talking with him for the next couple of years, I was amazed by what this man had experienced in his life.

By 1997, John was opening up to me more and more, and I was becoming fascinated by what he was telling me. I felt he had a story to tell that people would want to hear. I kept telling him to write his experiences down so they would not be lost forever. Finally, we arrived at a joint decision that I would do the writing.

We have all read about the heroic efforts of well-known people such as John F. Kennedy, General Douglas MacArthur and others. There is a difference, however, between John Mackowski's story and the stories of these famous people. They were, for the most part, important and influential people before events made them even more famous. They had been in charge of other people, and had some control over their own destiny. John's story is different. It is about an "average Joe" who came from a poor, but hard-working, blue collar family in New York City, who lived through the Depression, and who was drafted into military service in the 1940's just like millions of others.

I believe that people are very much a product of their environment and the importance of a strong family life, regardless of one's economic and social status, cannot be underestimated. The values instilled by family members, neighbors, teachers, policemen, local business people and other role models are very important to a young person's development. In this respect, John Mackowski was fortunate. As he was growing up, he was surrounded by honest, hard working people who taught him the difference between right and wrong, the value of hard work and the importance of standing up for what he believed. The values he learned as a young man would turn out to be very important to John's very survival.

This is not just a story about one young man named John Mackowski. It is also the story of the millions of other young Americans, men and women, who received very little training before being thrust into the horrors of World War II. The soldiers and sailors who served with John were hastily trained and given inferior, malfunctioning and outdated equipment with which to defend themselves. They were shipped out to the Philippines and ordered to fight a much larger and better equipped enemy while the rest of the country geared up for war.

In his book, *The Alamo of the Pacific*, Otis H. King compared the defenders of the Philippines to the defenders of the Alamo. From December 8, 1941 until May 6, 1942, these brave men and women, armed with obsolete and often inoperable equipment, blocked the Japanese armed forces from conquering the rest of the Pacific, including Australia. Out-numbered and poorly trained, they held two Japanese armies at bay for nearly six months. These men and women, including John Mackowski, gave the United States time to recover from the devastating attack on Pearl Harbor. There is no doubt that their heroic efforts changed the course of history.

POW-83 is the story of a foot soldier, a Private First Class (PFC) in the U.S. Army, who was ordered to surrender to a vicious and violent enemy. It is the story of a young man who somehow survived his day-to-day imprisonment, and through circumstances beyond his control, managed to escape from a horrendous ordeal. He lives with the scars, both physical and psychological, that he received at the hands of ruthless captors, as have so many other Americans - all of them heroes. The names have been changed of those POW's who fell victim to their circumstances and did not always act honorably.

Make no mistake. I do not claim that this book is one of the greatest books ever written about World War II, or that I have somehow become a great writer for having written it. I do believe, however, that John's story is an important part of history. With his permission and cooperation, we began a journey into his past, opening some old wounds, but also bringing back fond memories of his fellow soldiers who survived and came home, and those who did not.

PROLOGUE

It was August of 1944, and John could barely see the Japanese guards enter the guardhouse because his eyes were almost swollen shut from previous beatings. John was beginning to think that it was all over for him. He was sure that the guards had been ordered to beat him until he died. He had just said his prayers and was now prepared to die. There's nothing more these bastards can do to me because I am no longer afraid of death, he thought as the guards entered his cage.

The guards began their usual ritual. They yelled at him in Japanese and started to hit him with their fists and with a metal rod, and when he slumped down, they kicked him with their boots. There was a point when John just couldn't feel the pain anymore. He knew the guards were hitting him because he could feel the impact of their blows, but just couldn't feel the pain. He was thinking about his family and friends and how he probably wouldn't see them again. As he felt himself slipping away from the reality of a very cruel world, he managed to somehow muster the strength to show his captors one last act of defiance. It was just a faint smile, but it would show them that in spite of what they had done to him, they hadn't defeated him.

Chapter 1

GROWING UP IN GREENPOINT
Until March 1941

John Mackowski was born in the Greenpoint section of Brooklyn on January 27th, 1916. It was the same year that the Schaefer Brewery had moved its main operations to Kent Avenue and it is here, in "The Point" that John's story begins. For those of you who do not know much about New York City, Greenpoint is located in the northwest corner of Brooklyn near the East River and right across from Manhattan.

By the 1920's, Greenpoint was a melting pot made up mainly of newly-arrived immigrants and second generation people of Irish, Polish, German, Italian, Russian and Jewish descent. Although Prohibition had begun, it still seemed like there was a bar on every corner. The aroma of corned beef and cabbage, garlic, pasta and tomato sauce, and Polish kielbasa cooking on the stoves of various households filled the air in

13

Greenpoint.   Joining with the smell of freshly-baked breads and pastries from the Warsaw Bakery and the White Eagle Bakery, and the aroma of barley and hops from the brewery, they all mixed together to form a distinctive aroma that permeated the neighborhood all year long.

It was a time when people had ice boxes in their apartments instead of refrigerators and the ice man came on a horse-drawn wagon and carried the ice on his back up to the apartments. It was a time when men still came around on horse-drawn wagons to sell fruits, vegetables, cakes and pies, or to buy and sell used clothing and rags, and sometimes even to take the dead to the cemetery in a horse-drawn hearse.   There was a man who came around the Greenpoint neighborhood once a week to sharpen knives with a portable grinding wheel which he operated with a foot pedal. During hot summer evenings, the "watermelon man" would come around on his wagon, selling full watermelons or cut pieces that were sitting on large blocks of ice.

Every Saturday morning, the "potato man" came around in his wagon selling ten-pound bags of potatoes for 25 cents. People would yell down to the man from their apartment windows to send up 10 or 20 pounds. On some Saturdays, John would help the man out by carrying the potatoes up to the apartments. It was tough work, up and down the stairs of the apartment buildings all day long and carrying 10 or 20-pound bags of potatoes on his shoulder. At the end of a long and tiring day, John received a dollar for his efforts.

Many of these peddlers obtained their fruits and vegetables from the Walabout Market near the Brooklyn Navy Yard, where farmers from Long Island would come into the city to sell their produce. Trolley cars, powered by electricity and with their two sets of tracks firmly planted in the cobblestone streets of Manhattan Avenue, were still the main means of transportation in Greenpoint. The Nassau Trolley Line went from Nassau Avenue to Meeker Avenue; The Cross-town Line went from Manhattan Avenue to Court Street in Boro-Hall; The Greenpoint Line went from West Street at the ferry to Calvary Cemetery, and other trolley lines cris-crossed the neighborhood. Many of the people living in Greenpoint used these trolley lines to connect to the elevated train lines and the subways in order to get to their jobs in Manhattan.

The Mackowski's, like most other immigrant families in the neighborhood at the time, were poor, but somehow managed to get by with what they had. Most of the boys growing up in New York City in the 1920's wore knickers during most of the year, but when the summers arrived they wore shorts, and many went barefoot because shoes were so expensive. In addition to his one pair of leather shoes, which his father repaired because they couldn't afford to pay a shoemaker to fix them, John had a pair of high-top "Ked" sneakers. He wore them quite a bit during the summers, even to the Saints Cyril and Methodius Church on Sundays.

Many of the families in the neighborhood were large, and the Mackowski's were no exception. There were ten in the family, including John. His father, Edward, was a strong, well-built man who stood about 5 feet 9 inches tall. He had a heavy Polish accent, and although he didn't have much formal schooling, he could also speak very good German. This helped him get a job as a laborer at the Domino sugar factory on Wythe and Franklin Streets in Brooklyn, where the foreman was a

German immigrant. Edward could not read English very well, and he was also hard of hearing, so he often relied on young John to keep him up-to-date on what was happening in the world.

His mother, Mary, was born in the United States. Her parents, the Broski's, had come to the United States from Poland and had settled in Wilkes-Barre, Pennsylvania where she was born, also one of ten children. She stood about 5 feet 5 inches tall and was a very outspoken woman, as well as a hard worker. She not only took care of the family and the apartment, but also worked nights cleaning offices in Manhattan where she was paid five dollars a week.

John had three sisters, Florence and Irene, who were older, and Theresa, who was the youngest of the family. He had two brothers, Chester and Edward, both younger, and two half-brothers, Benjamin (Benny) and Zigmund (Mike), who were older than John and who were the sons of his mother, who had been widowed from a previous marriage.

When John was about six years old, his family was living in an apartment on the second floor of a three-story wood-frame apartment house on North 9th Street. As with most children at that age, he was very curious and always exploring the apartment looking to find something interesting. On one of his forays through the apartment, he happened to find on a table in the front room some matches that one of his brothers had left behind. Not knowing the danger involved, John decided that he would like to see the matches burn. He had seen his brothers use the matches to light cigarettes, so he decided he would try to light them up too.

He climbed up on the family's only sofa and positioned himself comfortably in the corner. It was one of those old-fashioned sofas that you would sink into when you sat down. He thought for a moment that maybe he shouldn't be playing with matches, but he wasn't too worried about getting caught because his father was at the other end of the apartment, in the kitchen, reading the Polish-language newspaper and having a cup of coffee. He knew that once his father began reading the paper, nothing would disturb him, so he began to strike the matches.

He struck the first match and watched the flame burn down almost to his fingers before he blew it out. That was easy, he thought, as he lit the second match, then the third and the fourth. He adjusted his position a little because he was beginning to sink down too low into the sofa. He was thoroughly enjoying looking at the flames of each match. Then it happened. As he struck the fifth match, the flame burned his fingers and he instinctively pulled his hand away and dropped the burning match. He didn't see where it went, but as luck would have it (or rather, as bad luck would have it), the burning match fell into the space between the cushion and the right arm of the couch. John frantically tried to find it, but he couldn't. He jumped off the sofa and looked under it, behind it, and behind the small table and lamp that was next to the sofa, but he still couldn't find the match. Ah, maybe it went out, he thought. Then he noticed a little smoke coming from between the cushion and the side of the sofa. Within seconds, a thick dark smoke began pouring out, and then he saw flames coming from the deep crevices of the couch. Now he knew he was in trouble. He had no choice. He had to tell his father, or the whole apartment building would surely burn down.

"Hey Dad, there's a fire in the couch!" he frantically yelled, as if he didn't know how it started. His father ran into the room, looked at the burning couch and turned to John.

"What the hell are you trying to do, Johnny, burn the whole building down? Get the hell out of the way!" his father shouted.

John watched as his father tried to put the fire out by beating on the couch with an old towel, but it didn't work. In fact, it seemed to have the opposite effect. It was almost as if his father was fanning the fire with the towel.

It wasn't long before the fire in the sofa really started to get going. The apartment was rapidly filling with an acrid smoke that was starting to burn John's eyes and throat. At that point, John's father, without saying another word, picked up one end of the sofa, pulled it across the room and placed it on the sill of the open window. John couldn't quite understand what his father was doing. He heard his father yell out the window for people to get away from the building. Then he pushed the couch out the window and it fell, still burning, onto the sidewalk below. His father's quick actions probably prevented the whole apartment building from catching on fire and burning down.

A man who was walking by the building saw what was happening, ran to the corner and pulled the fire alarm box. Within a minute or two, the unmistakable sounds of New York City fire engines could be heard. Before long, the firemen pulled up in front of the building and put out the fire in the sofa. John was watching everything from the front room window. He could hear his parents talking to the firemen explaining what had happened. John knew he was in for it as he saw his mother and father come back into the apartment building.

"You should thank God that no one was walking down the street when your father threw the couch out the window, because they surely would have been killed and it would all be your fault!" his mother told him.

"Don't you ever play with matches again! Do you hear me?" his father added.

"Yes, yes, I hear you. I'll never do it again," John sheepishly replied as his father whacked him a few times on the seat of his pants to reinforce his point. It took quite a long time before John's parents forgave him.

In the mid 1920's, the Mackowski family moved to a first-floor cold-water railroad-style apartment on the right side of a four-story, wood-sided grayish-blue apartment building at 317 Eckford Street, just off Greenpoint Avenue. There were two families on each floor, and both families had to share the one toilet area that consisted of only a commode. Each family took turns cleaning it every other week. There was no sink, bathtub or shower, so the family had to go to a public bath, located a few blocks away on Huron Street, at least once a week.

It was a typical railroad flat, with connecting rooms going from the front of the building to the rear. The kitchen was located towards the back. You had to pass through each of the three bedrooms to get to the front room. The main entrance was through the kitchen door, which had a pane of glass on the upper part. There was another entrance door to the apartment located towards the front of the building, but it was blocked with furniture. There was a combination gas stove in the kitchen for cooking and heating and the family used a portable gas heater in the winter to heat the back rooms. Light was provided by gas jets on the walls that were lit by a match. John often sat by these gaslights and read about the exploits of World War I pilots in a magazine called *Battle Aces*.

John's mother used a large soapstone tub and washboard to clean the family's clothes. They dried on a clothesline that went out of the kitchen window and was attached at the other end to another building. As the children grew older, John's mother began to send the laundry out to a commercial dry cleaner on Russell Street. When the laundry came back, she would soak the clothes in cold water to get the chemicals out, then hang them out to dry.

On the Mackowski side of the building, the Fitzgeralds lived on the second floor. They had a son, Paddy, who hung out with John. John's grandmother, Josephine Broski, and some of his uncles lived on the third floor. Every year, just before Lent on Saint Joseph's Day, the entire family, including many other relatives who lived elsewhere, gathered at his grandmother's apartment to celebrate her birthday and enjoy traditional Polish foods. One of his uncles, Uncle Lou, was a favorite of John's. He had been a sergeant in the Army and regularly entertained John and his siblings with stories of his experiences during World War I.

The O'Neal family lived on the fourth floor. They had two sons, Tommy and Jimmy, who were older than John and who hung out with John's half-brothers, Benny and Mike. On the other side of the building, the first-floor apartment remained vacant most of the time. A Russian Jewish family, whose father was a furrier in Manhattan, lived on the second floor. On the third floor was the Knidis family. They had two sons, Paulie and Mike, and an older daughter named Julie. On the fourth floor was an older couple who had no children and pretty much kept to themselves.

When John was about seven years old, he was playing around the new apartment. He picked up an old belt buckle and put it in his mouth. Somehow, he managed to half swallow it, and it became lodged in his throat. He couldn't talk and was having a very difficult time trying to breathe, but he managed to make his way into the kitchen where his mother was sitting. All he could do was point at his throat and make strange gurgling noises. He thought for sure that he was going to die.

When his mother turned around and saw him, John could see the look of fear on her face. She became very upset and didn't know quite what to do. She was screaming frantically at the top of her lungs. "Oh God, please help me! Oh God, Help! Somebody please help me!" Then she opened the kitchen door out to the hallway and began screaming. "Help! Help! Somebody help me! My son's choking!"

Just then, John's oldest brother, Benny, who was about 18 at the time, ran into the kitchen from one of the other rooms and yelled to John. "Bend over, Johnny!" When he did, his brother whacked him on the back, almost knocking him down, but nothing happened. Things were starting to get dark, and now John could not get any air, when Benny hit him on the back again. This time, the force of Benny's blow knocked John down to his knees. The belt buckle flew from his mouth onto the floor, and John started to breathe normally again. His mother let out a sigh and began yelling for all the world to hear. "Thank you God! Oh thank you God! Oh Benny! Oh Benny! You saved Johnny's life!" Then she began kissing John and Benny over and over again. After she calmed down a little, she gave John a good tongue-lashing and a few whacks on his behind.

John was no different than other youngsters growing up in the ethnic neighborhoods of New York City at that time. He sat on the front stoops of the buildings talking with his friends about their hopes and dreams and about what they wanted to do when they grew up. They stood around telling jokes and making farting sounds by putting their hands under one of their armpits and flapping their arm like a bird. They often walked to Winthrop Park, usually using the Nassau and Russell Street entrance, to check out what was going on. On Sundays during the summer months, a band would play in the park shelter for the residents of the neighborhood.

There were other places in the neighborhood where John and his friends would go. One of these was McCarren Park, which was by far the biggest of all the parks in the neighborhood. It had everything. There were a basketball court, baseball fields, handball courts, swings, a running track and even some tennis courts. There were also two other, smaller parks in the neighborhood, one on Franklin Street and the other on Dupont Street, that had just a few swings and some tennis courts.

Walking down Manhattan Avenue in those days was an experience. It was a thriving community of small stores and shops. There was Woolworth's "5 and 10 cent" store and Honig's Department Store. Across from Saint

Anthony's Church was Cushman's Bakery, which made great "black and white" cakes. On the same side of the street as Saint Anthony's were the Butler Grocery Store, Bohack's and the Trunz Pork Store. Not far away was the Warsaw Bakery and Simon's Bicycle Shop. There were numerous "mom and pop" clothing stores and several large supermarket chain stores, like the A&P and Gristedes. There were also several movie theaters — the American on Manhattan Avenue, the RKO on Manhattan and Calyer, the Meserole on Manhattan Avenue between Meserole and Norman Avenues, the Eagle on Eagle Street and the Nassau Theater on Nassau Street. Manhattan Avenue was lined with banks. There was the Greenpoint Savings Bank at Calyer, the Irving Trust Bank on the other side of the street at Greenpoint Ave., the National City Bank at Noble, the Corn Exchange Bank and the Manhattan Bank. Directly across from the Irving Trust Bank, also on the corner, was a cigar and newspaper store.

One day, when John was about 10 years old, he was walking down Manhattan Avenue between Milton and Greenpoint Avenues when he passed by a group of older boys (who were probably no older than thirteen or so). As he walked passed the group, one of them threw a small stone that hit John square in the back of the head. The pain was so sharp that John started crying. As he turned around to see who threw the stone, he noticed that the other guys were all laughing at him. At first, he didn't understand why they were laughing. When he looked down at the sidewalk, he saw that the stone had broken in two and he, too, started to laugh, although he did have quite a bump on the back of his head for a few days.

Youngsters passed the time by playing games like "Johnny Ride the Pony", "Pitching Pennies", "Stoop Ball" and "Punch Ball." On Halloween, they would fill old socks with ground chalk and go around hitting other boys with it. Most of them were smart enough to wear their coats inside out on Halloween so they wouldn't get in trouble with their parents for getting their coats full of chalk.

The Election Day bonfires in Greenpoint were something to remember. Boys would gather scrap wood, wooden crates, used and broken 2x4's, and anything else they could find that would burn, and pile it up in the middle of the Street, light it and watch the asphalt melt. Empty cans of Carnation evaporated milk could also be used to pass the time. The boys would crunch the cans into the crevices between the soles and heels of their shoes. As they walked down the street with the old crushed cans firmly lodged under their shoes, it made a sound like horses going down cobblestone streets.

It was a good time to grow up in New York City. There wasn't much crime to speak of, and people did a lot of walking in those days. Although most families had enough money to get by, they didn't have extra money to spend on such luxuries as cars.

Then there was the Ace Billiards and Bowling Alley, located two flights of stairs up from the street and above the American Theater (pronounced "The-ay-ter") on Manhattan Avenue just off the corner of Greenpoint Avenue, next to the old 94th Precinct. Ace Billiards was owned by Pete Atchison. He had four children: three sons — Pete Jr., Jimmy and Tommy — and a daughter named Dotty. There were only four or six lanes in the bowling alley. John remembered bowling here with his friends one

Saturday afternoon and somehow managing to make a 7-10 split.

The Mackowski family moved to another apartment building in Greenpoint at 195 Kent Street, between Manhattan Avenue and Oakland Street. It was another railroad apartment, but somehow it seemed roomier than their previous apartments, and the building was much cleaner and better maintained.

John was becoming a pretty active kid who was always doing something to keep busy. He spent a lot of time hanging out with his friends in the vicinity of Newton Creek. The creek was very polluted at the time, and it was not uncommon to see oil slicks, pieces of wood, and even butchered animal parts floating on top of the water. At that time, the VanInstine Rendering plant, which was located alongside the creek, discarded animal by-products directly into the creek. There were also several oil refineries — Standard Oil, Vedol-Tydol Oil, Paragon Oil, Esso Oil, Richfield Oil, Sun Oil, and others — that regularly polluted the creek. The creek was so polluted that the Russell #1, a small tugboat that regularly plied the waters of the creek, had to move extremely slow so that it would not stir up the muck from the bottom.

The O'Leary Sawmill and Lumberyard was also located on Newton Creek. The sawmill regularly received large quantities of logs that were delivered by a ship that still had sails on it. The employees of the mill would unload the logs from the boats into the water, bind several logs together and store them right in the creek. Now and then, there would be a couple of loose logs in the creek and some scrap lumber on the creek edge.

One summer day, John, his younger brother Chester and two of his friends, Paddy and Tommy, were sitting on the stoop in front of 195 Kent Street. They were talking about what they were going to do for the day when someone came up with the bright idea of building a raft to sail in the creek. With a hammer and a few nails requisitioned from Tommy's apartment, the four would-be sailors headed out for the creek. They walked over to Manhattan Avenue and headed north towards the creek, passing the trolley barn, the coal yard and the old rope factory before coming to the creek's edge near O'Leary's Sawmill and Lumberyard. It didn't take them long to nail a couple of boards across some loose logs to make the makeshift raft.

Even though the hot summer day seemed to make the Newtown Creek even more foul-smelling and dirtier than it usually was, it did not stop the young adventurers from pushing their raft out into the water, which was about four to six feet deep. John, Paddy and Tommy went out on the raft, while Chester stayed on shore.

The three were using 2x4 pieces of lumber as oars and poles to move the raft along. Somehow, during this maiden voyage, the raft seemed to be listing a little to the port side, so John decided he would move from the left side of the raft to the right side. As he stood up to move, he slipped on one of the wet and greasy logs, lost his footing and fell off the raft into the creek. He came up quickly and grabbed onto one of the logs as Paddy and Tommy tried to maneuver the raft towards shore. As they neared the shoreline, John's feet finally touched the creek bottom and he walked up the bank. As he stood there in the hot summer sun, he was covered with oil and other multi-colored goo from the creek. After his two friends beached the raft, they walked up the bank to where John and his brother Chester were standing.

"Hey Johnny, what the hell is that stink?" Paddy asked, with laughter punctuating his sentence.

"Jesus, you smell like an old rotten egg fart," Tommy added, with a hint of laughter in his voice as well.

"What's Mom gonna say when she sees you? Boy, you're really gonna get in trouble this time," Chester added.

"Me? What about you? You were with us. You're gonna be in trouble, too," John told his younger brother.

As the four walked back towards Kent Street, they were talking and laughing about what happened and trying to decide what John was going to tell his mother when he got home.

"Johnny, what you gonna tell your mother?" Tommy asked.

"I don't know what the heck I'm gonna tell her. All I know is that I can't tell her what really happened," John said.

"I can just see it now. Hey, Mom! Me, Tommy and Paddy were sailing on a raft in the Newton Creek and I fell off," he added.

"Then what you gonna do?" Tommy asked.

"Well, I'd better not tell her what really happened, or we'll all get in trouble, not just me," he replied.

"Why would we get in trouble?" Paddy asked.

"Because you were with me you dope. That's why." John said. "Besides that, she'd never believe it. And if she did believe it, I'd get in trouble for sailing on the raft." He added.

"Then what you gonna tell her?" asked Chester.

"I'll tell her that we were walking along the creek when I slipped and accidentally fell in. That should be believable," John said.

"Sounds good to me," Tommy said, and the other two nodded their agreement. So he stuck to the story about accidentally falling into the creek. It worked, but his poor mother had to wash his clothes several times to get the stains and the horrible smell out of them.

During the summer months, when he was bored, John would often go on long walks by himself to Central Park. He would start out from Kent Street, walk across the Manhattan Avenue Bridge to the Queensboro (59th Street) Bridge, then across the East River to 59th Street in Manhattan, and then on to Central Park. One afternoon, John decided to take a walk down to the East River by himself to watch the bigger kids swim from a dock located next to the fireboat station on Noble Street. From the docks of Greenpoint, it seemed that Manhattan was only a stone's throw away across the river. It was a favorite pastime of many of the guys to "skim" a rock across the river and try to hit the other side. When John arrived at the dock, he could see the fireboat Hewitt tied up at the fireboat station on the next dock over. While he was sitting on the side of the dock looking at Manhattan and watching the guys jumping off the dock into the East River, one of the older guys pointed to the edge of the dock and said, "Hey, look at that. Did ya ever see anything like that before?" A lot of the older guys were standing at the edge of the dock looking over into the water saying things like, "That's the biggest one I ever saw," "What the hell is that thing?" and "Look at the colors!"

Well, John's curiosity got the best of him. He stood up, walked right to the edge of the dock and bent over to see what they were looking at. One of the older boys got behind him and pushed him into the river. As he fell face first into the cold East River, John knew that he had "been had" by the older boys. It had all been just a trick to get one of the younger boys to the edge, and John just happened to be the first to go over. Luckily, he had held his breath before he hit the water. He quickly popped up to the surface and started to dog paddle to the side of the pier.

He managed to grab onto a rope and hold on for dear life. After he caught his breath, and with some help from some of the older boys (one of whom had probably pushed him in), he pulled himself up onto the dock. As he was standing there, fully clothed and dripping wet, one of the older guys came over to him and asked: "Hey kid, what happened to you? How did ya get in the river?"

"Someone pushed me in," John replied.

"Well, I guess you learned how to swim the hard way," the guy said, chuckling as he walked away towards Noble Street. John had learned a valuable lesson that day. He didn't know then just how valuable a lesson it was going to be, but being able to dog paddle in the water would save his life one day.

John received a pretty good education from the schools in New York City. He attended P.S. #126 Elementary and Junior High School on Meserole Avenue in Greenpoint, where the "Boys Entrance" and the "Girls Entrance" were clearly marked in stone above two entrances to the school. The boy's entrance was on the left side of the building and the girl's entrance was on the right side. The school's name was later changed to the John Erickson Junior High School in honor of the man who had designed and built the Monitor during the Civil War. John had some good teachers at this school who were very important in shaping his future.

During this time, New York City was embarking on a major expansion of the subway system, building a tunnel for a new subway line, the "GG" train, which would run through Greenpoint. The new line was to be part of the "IND" or Independent line. There was construction debris and airshaft holes about 15 feet deep, all along Manhattan Avenue, one of the major thoroughfares in Greenpoint, and the avenue that the trolley cars ran on.

When he was about 14 years old, John was walking along Manhattan Avenue on a hot, summer day when he saw a group of boys standing around the eight-foot opening at the top of one of the air shafts. There was also a group of younger boys, nine or ten years old, playing around it. He saw a neighborhood bully, whom John only knew by the nickname "Red" come along with a couple of his friends and stop by the air shaft.

As John walked over to see what was going on, he heard "Red", who was about 16 years old, tell the younger boys, "I'll throw a nickel down the shaft and if one of you guys goes down to get it, you can keep it."

"I'll do it," one of the younger boys said.

"And I'll go with him," another one told Red. John didn't know the younger boys, but he watched as they jumped down to the bottom of the airshaft where it was very sandy.

"We got it!" one of the young boys yelled up.

"I can see that," Red yelled back.

"OK, we're coming up," one of them said.

"I don't think so," Red said.

"What do ya mean?" one of the boys said.

"Cause I'm not letting you up. You can stay down there forever as far as I'm concerned." Red told them.

"Come on, Red. Let us up," the two young boys pleaded with Red.

"Comm on, Red. We'll give you the nickel back if you let us up," one of them said, and then they both started crying. At that point, John couldn't stand it any more. He walked over to Red.

"OK, you've had your fun. Let 'em up," John said.

"Why don't you mind your own goddamn business," Red said.

"Don't you see how scared they are? They're only little kids. Why don't you let them up?" John asked.

There was no answer from Red. He and his friends were having a great time at the expense of the two younger boys and were ignoring John's request. Red simply looked down at the two boys.

"You ain't never getting up. You'll probably die in there," Red told them, laughing all the time.

"Please Red. Let us up," the boys begged.

"What are you gonna do now? Call your mommy?" Red said. At that point, John had had enough of Red. He walked over and stood right in front of him.

"Let them up before you get in trouble," John said.

"Fuck you!" was Red's reply.

"Can't you see they're crying?" John said, trying to elicit some sympathy from Red.

"Why don't you mind your own business and go take a freaking hike," was Red's reply.

"Don't listen to him, Red," one of Red's friends yelled out.

"OK, you've made your point. You scared the hell out of them, so let them up!" John said.

"Why don't you try and make me," Red replied.

"I said, let them up!" John yelled right in Red's face.

31

"Make me!" Red said again, with his friends egging him on. It was now up to John to put up or shut up. He and Red were nose to nose. Red pushed John and said, "I told you to get the hell out of here. Now beat it before I beat the shit out of you."

One push quickly led to another, and pretty soon the two boys were fighting right in the middle of Manhattan Avenue, holding the trolley cars up. Finally, a conductor stepped off one of the trolleys and yelled out in a heavy Irish brogue: "You two lads! Get the hell out of the middle of the street and do your fighting on the sidewalk."

At one point, Red threw a roundhouse punch; John ducked and Red's punch missed, but John landed a hard right just above Red's heart, knocking Red backwards over the fender of a car, which immediately took the fight out of him. Red's friends yelled out, "Don't take that crap from him! Hit him back Red! Hit him!" They were urging him to keep fighting, but John could tell that Red didn't want to fight anymore.

John then turned to Red's two buddies and said, "If you guys want a piece of me, I'll fight both of you, too," but they declined. There were no takers for John's offer. As Red and his friends left, the two younger boys managed to climb out of the airshaft and thanked John for his help. The boys kept the nickel for their trouble and John received a couple of bruises for his efforts.

John had quite a few other fistfights when he was young. He had lost a couple when he was very young, but by the time he was a teenager he could really hold his own. On one occasion, he saw an older boy beating up his younger brother, and he stepped in and beat up the older boy. It seemed that he was always fighting bigger and older boys than himself. His older brother Benny gave him the nickname "moxie" because he had a lot of guts.

In December of 1930, several oil refineries located along Newton Creek were destroyed in a spectacular blaze. and the Greenpoint Ferry, which had been running since 1790, made its final trip to Manhattan in 1933. By the mid-1930, the Depression was in full swing. People were losing their jobs and couldn't find new ones. Depression hit the Mackowski family hard, just like it hit millions of other American families. John's father, Edward, could only find work two days a week, but somehow the family still managed to get by. His mother would make huge pots of thick soup using marrow bones and chuck meat, to which she added rice and barley to make a thick base, and usually some vegetables. Sometimes the family had fresh bread to go along with the soup.

After graduating from P.S. 126 Junior High in Greenpoint, John began attending Grover Cleveland High School in the Ridgewood section of Queens. His mother gave him twenty cents a day for food and for trolley fare. In order to have some change left over for the end of the week, he often walked the three miles to school, rather than take the trolley. He had several part-time jobs while in junior high and high school. Sometimes, he would take his little red wagon over to O'Leary's Sawmill and to the other factories near Newtown Creek to look for scrap wood. He would cut it up into stove-size pieces and sell it on Saturdays as kindling for coal stoves. He would get about fifteen cents for a burlap bag full of kindling. He often made a dollar or two doing this.

He worked at John's Butcher Shop on Manhattan Avenue, near Huron Street, as a delivery boy. He delivered packages to customers on Saturdays and earned about a dollar and a half. If he received any tips, he turned them over to his mother. In fact, he gave all of the money he earned to his mother and she gave him twenty cents a day for school and an extra quarter a week for himself.

Next, he worked as a delivery boy for George Buss' Butcher Shop on Kent Street. He worked every day after school and on Saturdays for two dollars a week. George Buss was a very nice man who took a personal interest in John. One Christmas, George saw that John was wearing a rather light jacket, so he took John over to the Army-Navy Store on the corner of Manhattan and Greenpoint Avenues and bought him a gray, white and black checkered winter coat for four dollars as a Christmas present. Occasionally, when Mr. Buss needed to take cash out of the store, John would walk him home to his apartment at the end of Greenpoint Avenue when Mr. Buss' assistant, Charlie Dombrowski, couldn't accompany him.

When John worked at the butcher shop, construction of the new subway line was also in progress. Unfortunately for the storeowners on Manhattan Avenue, particularly those dealing in food products, the construction was causing large numbers of rats to come out of the airshafts at night to forage for food. Many times during the construction, George Buss and Charlie Dombrowski would sit outside of the store at night and shoot the rats with a .22 caliber rifle.

In order to earn some extra cash, John boarded the Borden Avenue trolley carrying a watering can, a spade and grass-clippers, and headed to the Second Calvary Cemetery in Queens. He would walk up and down the cemetery looking for people who were visiting the graves and he would ask them if they wanted him to water the grave site, cut the grass or whatever. He would take what they gave him. Usually, it was fifteen cents to a quarter, but once a man gave him three dollars.

As the Depression wore on, John's parents could no longer afford to give him the twenty cents a day to get to school. He was doing his chores at home, had several part-time jobs and he often didn't get to bed until well after ten o'clock at night. There wasn't much time left for his studies. He started to fail most of his courses, so he quit high school in 1933, his junior year, to look for a full-time job to help out the family. His brother Mike found him a job as a driver's helper at the Morgan Cleaners, a commercial cleaning plant located on Morgan Avenue in Greenpoint, where he earned five dollars a week. The hours were long, from 10:00 AM to 10:00 PM, six days a week. He only stayed on this job for about four months.

He then became a shipping clerk at a manufacturing plant in Long Island City that made various automobile accessories. By then, the National Recovery Act had been passed, and the minimum wage was forty cents an hour. He was earning sixteen dollars a week. He gave his mother twelve dollars, and he kept four for himself. As the 1930's moved along, the economic situation of his family started to improve. More money was coming into the family. His sisters were working, and his two half-brothers, Benny and Mike, had gone out on their own. His former high school football coach, Dan Goody, now with Boys High in Brooklyn, tried to entice him to come back and finish high school. The coach promised he would get him a scholarship to Temple University, but John declined the offer.

On Sunday afternoons during the fall, John and his friends played sandlot football. They played an Army team from Fort Totten, the Bulldogs from Ridgewood Queens, the Red Raiders from Flushing and other teams, mostly from Queens and Long Island. He was once paid $3.00 for playing a game in Ridgewood because the attendance was so good. At one of the games, a friend of John's Chet Legczak, introduced him to a fellow Stuyvesant H.S. student named Ed Kolman, who later went on to play for the Chicago Bears.

It was now 1936, and President Roosevelt's State of the Union message was full of doom and gloom. Japan had walked out of the Naval Limitation talks; Italian troops were marching through Ethiopia; and the Nazi's had assassinated the Austrian Chancellor. A month later, Roosevelt was asking Congress for the biggest naval appropriation in history for "the country's prudent self-defense." The newspapers were filled with anti-war stories: of 50,000 WWI veterans staging a "March for Peace" around the White House, and of school children staging classroom strikes to demand "schools not battleships." A wave of isolationist sentiment was sweeping across America even as Mussolini was staging his victory parades in Rome, Hitler was calling another half-million Germans into the armed forces, and Japan was sending additional troops into China.

A dollar went pretty far in those days. John was going out on the town on weekends and having a great time. There was no incentive to go back to school. He hung out with guys named Tommy, Walter, Lou, Jake and Eddie, and other guys with nicknames like "Lefty",

"Chester the mad dog" and "Boris Karloff." Their main hangout was Chris Schultz's Tavern on the corner of Calyer and Lorimer Streets. They liked it because a tall glass of Schlitz beer was only a nickel, even though the tavern was located only a few blocks down from the Shaeffer Brewery. They also hung out in the newly formed Polish-American Club on Java Street. From these two locations, they would head out to dance halls and other taverns. John was still pretty much a rough guy. Although he doesn't remember starting any fights, he rarely walked away from one. He would become involved in fights outside of the New National Dance Hall on Driggs Avenue, as well as other local dance halls, often coming to the aid of his buddies, particularly Lou, who always started fights when he got drunk.

There was another side to his character: John rarely refused a challenge. After spending most of the evening and early morning hours in the Freeman Street Tavern, the now-20-year-old John Mackowski was heading home with Tommy and Lou. As they were walking home down the nearly deserted streets, John said, "You know, its so quiet around here, I could run around the block in my underpants and no one would say anything."

"You're full of shit," Tommy said.

"Put your money where your mouth is," John said.

"I'll give you a buck if you do it," Tommy said. Well, John did it. He ran around the block in his underpants and collected the dollar from Tommy. There were no cops around, and no one seemed to notice.

Another night, he was in the Freeman Street Tavern with Tom and Teddy where Tom's brother, Vinny, happened to be the bartender. They always went there when Vinny was the bartender because they would get a couple of extra "buy backs" (free rounds from the bartender) during the evening. John, Ted and Tom were sitting in a booth with two young women and they were talking about how John would take on almost any dare. One of the young women didn't believe him and said, "I dare you to stand up and drop your pants."

"Jeez, don't dare him to do that! He's gonna get us all kicked out of here!" Tom told her. Just then, without another word being spoken, John jumped up on top of the table and dropped his pants (however he still had his underwear on). He didn't pull his pants back up until after Vinny came around the bar and told him, "Hey, Johnny! Pull your pants up and behave yourself or I'll throw the five of you out of here, including my dopey brother!"

On the morning of December 13, 1937, the newspapers and radio stations were reporting that an American gunboat, the USS Panay, which had left the city of Nanking, China, had been sunk in the Yangtze River by Japanese warplanes. Two American sailors and an Italian journalist had been killed in the unprovoked attack. The news of this incident outraged the American public and it looked, for a short time, like the United States would be going to war with Japan. The Japanese government avoided war with the U.S., however, by agreeing to the demand for a formal apology and compensation of over two million dollars. There were heated discussions about the incident in American homes, workplaces and bars, and many Americans, including John, couldn't understand why President Roosevelt was letting the Japanese get away with attacking and sinking one of our navy ships. By Christmas of 1937, however, the incident was considered closed and the stories disappeared from the newspapers.

It was now 1938, and everything seemed to be going along just fine for John. He had just started driving an oil truck at night for the Meehan Oil Company of Long Island City, delivering #6 heating oil to the big apartment houses, factories and hotels, including the Vanderbilt Hotel on Park Avenue in Manhattan. In January, John was an usher at his friend Jake's wedding. After the wedding, everyone went to the Leviton Company's Reception Hall on Diamond Street in Greenpoint, which was regularly used by Leviton's employees for such affairs. While there, he met a young woman by the name of Opaline Walendziak. John had no idea at the time that this lovely young woman would eventually become his partner for life.

Towards the end of the wedding reception, John and Tom left the hall early with Opaline and her friend Jean. All four headed to Chris Schultz' Tavern, which was only about five or six blocks away. It was a very cold night. Tommy and the two young ladies had overcoats on, but John was wearing only his rented tuxedo. As they walked along, John and Tommy acted like fools, running and jumping over fire hydrants and generally having a great time, finally arriving at the tavern where the four enjoyed the rest of the evening together. John and Opaline talked all night and really seemed to hit it off. As the foursome was leaving the bar, Tom said, "Hey John, you walk Jean home and I'll take Opaline home."

"Not on your life, buddy; I don't know what you're doing, but I'm taking Opal home and that's that," John replied. He walked Opaline home to her third floor apartment at 110 India Street where she lived with her parents, Alexander and Bertha. Tom walked Jean home to her apartment on Freeman Street. For the next year or so, John and Opaline saw each other at least once a week, usually on Sundays. It was pretty tough to see each other more often because John worked nights, six days a week. They had a favorite song, "Apple Blossom Time," sung by the Andrew Sisters.

John and Opal began talking about getting married. John had kind of "unofficially" asked Opaline if she would marry him, because he didn't want to waste money on a ring if she was going to turn him down. Opal had "unofficially" agreed to marry John, but said that if they were to get engaged, she would like it to be on her birthday, which was February 9th. John began saving for an engagement ring. He wanted to ask Opaline for her hand in marriage, but he wanted to do it right. John's brother Mike gave him the name of a jeweler in the diamond district in Manhattan, so on the afternoon of February 9th, 1939, John went over to the jeweler on 45th Street. John had to be 'buzzed in' and escorted to the jeweler's booth. He bought a three-quarter carat ring for $350. and then headed back to Brooklyn.

He was working the night shift that night, as usual, delivering for the Meehan Oil Company. Between deliveries, he drove the truck over to Opal's building, parked it in front and went up to her apartment. When he knocked on the door, Opal answered.

"Happy birthday!" John said.

"What are you doing here? I thought you were supposed to be at work," she said.

"Happy birthday again, and by the way, I have the ring. Will you marry me?" John nervously asked. Opal whispered "Yes," and quickly ushered John into her room where she gave him a big kiss and a hug and asked him to put the ring on her finger. Then they both walked out and announced their engagement to her parents and showed them the ring.

John and Opaline often went to the New York Paramount Theater in Manhattan to see a movie and a show. The evening's entertainment usually started off with music by a big band, followed by a short vaudeville act, and then ended with a movie. John had the habit of taking his shoes off in the movies. On one occasion, as he was taking his right shoe off, it somehow fell beneath the row of seats in front of them and he couldn't find it in the darkness. Opal started laughing at his plight. Soon, the people in front of them were laughing, too, and John was getting ticked off. After about five minutes of searching on his hands and knees, he finally located the shoe and started to laugh himself. They enjoyed the rest of that evening which featured the Sammy Kaye orchestra whose slogan was "Swing and sway with Sammy Kaye."

During another outing to the Paramount Theater, the Tommy Dorsey band was playing. As an added attraction, there was a comedian named Red Skelton who was doing an imitation of a guy down on his luck whom he called "Freddie the Freeloader." Freddie was drinking 'sloe-gin,' and the more he drank, the drunker he acted. John thought the comedian was very funny. He was laughing even after Red Skelton had finished his act. The movie began after a short intermission, but John could still not stop laughing, even during some of the sad scenes. People nearby were looking around and giving John and Opal dirty looks. Opal, in turn, would poke John in the side to get him to stop laughing, but he couldn't. Even on the subway ride home on the "F" and

41

"GG" trains, John was still laughing at Red Skelton's antics.

On September 1, 1939, the newspapers and radio stations were reporting that German troops had marched into Poland. Forty-eight hours later, a general war broke out in Europe. That Sunday night, September 3rd, the passenger liner Athenia was sunk by a German U-boat as she steamed out to cross the Atlantic, packed with refugees from the war. The specter of the Lusitania was raised by the loss of twenty-two American lives, but President Roosevelt in a nationwide broadcast reassured the country that the U.S. Navy would now be deployed in the Atlantic to "keep war from our firesides."

By 1940, the German Blitzkrieg was in full swing with Germany carrying out lightning invasions of Norway, Holland, Belgium and France. During the summer of 1940, around the same time as the German army entered Paris, John's sister Florence let him use her husband Ed's car to drive Opal up to Connecticut to visit her grandmother. Opal asked John if she could drive and John let her, even though she didn't have a driver's license. As they were heading north on the Bronx River Parkway, they stopped at the tollbooth at the New York City line. As she started to move the car forward from the tollbooth, Opal repeatedly stalled the car. She finally managed to get the car moving forward, but it was bucking like a horse that was being ridden for the first time. There was a State Trooper parked alongside the road just north of the tollbooth, and he was watching them as they pulled out. John thought that the Trooper would stop them for sure, but Opal finally managed to get the car moving and the Trooper didn't budge.

In October of 1940, local Draft Board #194 notified John that his draft number, 158, had been selected from the "fish bowl" meaning that he would be drafted into the army at some future date. He was somewhat downhearted at this because he had finally found someone whom he cared for very much, and he was afraid that if he was drafted he would lose her. There was a rush of volunteers joining the various military services at the time, and he had not been called up earlier, so he had been putting the possibility of being drafted in the back of his mind.

Everyone was talking about what was going on in the rest of the world. Some of John's friends, including Lou Malecki, were joining the military services. The newspapers were filled with stories of the successes of Germany, Italy and Japan. It looked like Germany was winning the war in Europe. The Italians were in North Africa and the Japanese were taking over countries in Indo-China. On October 30, 1940, the New York Daily News reported that Franklin Roosevelt, while speaking before an election year audience in Boston said, "I have said this before, but I shall say it again and again and again: Your boys are not going to be sent to any foreign wars!"

Working for the oil company was seasonal work, and now that he was going to get married, john knew he'd better start looking for a permanent year-round job to support a wife and family. Little did he know what effect his next job would have on his life. Sometime towards the end of February of 1941, John received a "Greetings" notice from his local draft board ordering him to report for duty on March 25, 1941.

Other couples whom John and Opal knew had been getting married earlier than they planned because, at that time, married men were still exempt from the draft. John talked it over with Opal for quite a while, but they decided that since the draft was only supposed to be for a year, they would take their time to get married when John returned from the Army.

Chapter 2

YOU'RE IN THE ARMY NOW
March 1941

On March 24th, the night before he was to report to the draft board, John and Opal spent a quiet night together at her parents' apartment. They listened to music on the radio, and even heard a song called "I'll be Back in a Year, Darling." Opal turned to John and in a voice that was almost a whisper, asked, "Johnny, what's going to happen to us? Do you think we're going to war?"

"Don't worry," John replied softly, "I'll only be in the Army for a year or so, and then I'll be home." It was around 10 o'clock when he said his good-byes to Opal's parents. Then he and Opal walked slowly to the apartment door because they both knew that it might be a long, long time before they saw each other again. He kissed her gently on the lips several times and then said, "Don't worry. Nothing is going to happen. You'll see! I'll be back in Greenpoint before you know it."

He turned and walked down the stairs and onto the street, heading back to his family's apartment at 213 Kent Street. All sorts of ideas were going through his head on the way back. I wonder what it's gonna be like? I wonder if I'll meet someone from the neighborhood? Gee, I'm really gonna miss Opal, he thought. Before he knew it, he arrived at his building. He had never thought about it before, but now he was thinking about how nice it was to just come home to this building and his family's apartment. He thought about how he had taken it for granted all of these years that his parents, brothers and sisters were always there for him. He was gonna miss them, too. He sat down at the kitchen table and talked to his parents and his brothers and sisters for a while, then went to bed. It would be his last night in his own bed for quite some time.

Early the next morning, John's father, brothers and sisters stopped by his bed between 5:45 AM and 6:15 AM to say good-bye on their way to work. When John got out of bed around 6:30 AM, his mother was the only one home. He shaved, washed up, got dressed and packed a little ditty bag with some toiletries, extra underwear, socks and some other clothes. When John walked into the kitchen, he was a little surprised when he saw that his mother had made him a big breakfast of bacon, eggs, toast and coffee. After he finished his meal, he told his mother not to worry about him. He kissed her on the cheek, told her he loved her and headed off to the draft board around 8:30 AM.

John walked out of the apartment building, turned left and walked down to Oakland Street, carrying all of his possessions in a small ditty bag. Then he made a right on Meserole and walked his three final blocks as a civilian to Local Draft Board #194, which was located in the basement of John Erickson Junior High School. When he arrived at the school, he paused for a moment and looked at the sign over the entrance door. The words "Boys Entrance" were carved in the stone. Boy, did that sign bring back memories! He remembered his sixth-grade teacher, Mrs. Billings, who really made him toe the line. During a test one day, someone in the class was talking and Mrs. Billings assumed that John was the guilty one.

"John, there is no talking during tests. Keep Quiet!" she yelled. Because she embarrassed him in front of his classmates, John decided to fail the test on purpose. When he handed in his test, the teacher looked at it and said, "John, why are you doing this! I know you know the answers to these questions. After lunch, you come back here and take this test again. You're not leaving here today until you pass this test." She made him take the test again and he scored a 95 on it. Mrs. Billings seemed to have a soft spot in her heart for John.

Then there was his homeroom teacher, Miss Valentine, who caught him acting up in class one day. She made him write five hundred times on the blackboard: "Education begins with self control." These two teachers saw potential in John and recommended him for a rapid advance class in which he took two grades in one year. Because of the dedication of these and other teachers at this school, John graduated from junior high school when he was only fourteen years old.

For a moment, John wished he was back at school. Life seemed a lot simpler back then. Unfortunately, it was 1941 and he had just been drafted. He opened the door and went down the stairs, where he saw a bunch of other guys just standing around and sitting on some cheap, wooden folding chairs in a large room in the basement. He didn't know any of them personally, but he had seen some of them around the neighborhood.

It wasn't long before the small room became filled with about 25 guys who were either standing against the wall in the crowded basement or sitting on small wooded folding chairs. All of them were holding little ditty bags, and some were smoking cigarettes and/or reading the morning editions of the New York Daily News or the Mirror. After about 20 minutes, a balding older man in his 60's, wearing glasses and a slightly crumpled dark-colored suit, came in the room and called off the names one by one. Everyone who was supposed to be there had shown up. The older man then told the group, "OK! Pick up all of your stuff. Go up the stairs and get on the bus that's parked right outside the side door. Don't leave any of your crap in the room. Good luck."

"Bull shit!" one of the guys yelled out as they headed out of the room. The man followed them up the stairs and watched the group load onto the bus, which was a regular civilian charter-type bus. Then he walked up to the open front door of the bus and told the driver: "OK! Take off and don't make any stops."

It didn't take long before the bus arrived in front of the Jamaica Armory, where they could see an Army sergeant standing in front of the huge wooden entrance doors. The sergeant walked over to the stopped bus and in a normal voice said, "All right you guys, get out of the bus and form up in two lines in front of me." When they did, he quickly ushered them into the armory for their physical examinations.

After completing what seemed like a mountain of paperwork, the men were moved along from room to room, each occupied by a doctor. The doctors checked their blood pressure, weight, hearing, eyes, etc. Everyone was just standing around outside of the rooms waiting their turn to be examined. At one point, John was told to go upstairs for another test. He was getting impatient, so he decided to run up the stairs. As he started up the stairs, taking two steps at a time, one of the sergeants in the armory saw him and yelled, "Hey you! Walk. There's no running in here!"

The sergeant probably thought that John was trying to raise his heartbeat by running up the stairs. In any case, after a couple of hours, John and the other men were notified that they had all passed their physicals with flying colors. John and the others were brought into what appeared to be a company room on the first floor of the armory, and were sworn into the Army by a young lieutenant. After swearing them in, the lieutenant told them, "You're in the Army now and from now on, we'll tell you when to get up, when to go to bed and when to take a shit." Then he told one of the sergeants to take the group outside, where they were loaded onto a green Army bus and taken to Camp Upton on Long Island, which had been the main debarking point for new recruits during World War I. The group stayed at Camp Upton for about a week to complete their processing. The Army gave them another physical examination, issued them some Army uniforms and equipment, taught them how to march in formation and completed another round of what seemed like endless paperwork. John also caught a rather nasty cold during his short stay there.

The men were taken to get their first Army haircuts. It was kind of odd to see the changes in some of the guys, many of whom were typical wisecracking New Yorkers. When their hair was cut off, it was almost as if they underwent a personality change. It seemed to John like the short haircut had more of an effect on them than when they were sworn in at the armory.

During the down time that the group had, the guys would sit around and talk about where they thought they would be going and what kind of jobs they would be assigned to by the Army. The main rumor circulating was that the entire group was going to be sent to Fort Hood in Texas for basic training. When the orders finally came, however, John found out that he was going to Fort Belvoir in Virginia, where he was to receive his Army basic training as well as additional training to be a combat engineer.

At Fort Belvoir, John hooked up with five guys from New York City: Tom Mullins, Bill Lawler and Bill Longran, all of Irish descent, Gene Kowalski of Polish descent, and Fred Miller, who had been born in Germany. Miller had come to the United States after having served some time in the German Army.

Tom Mullins was a tall, well-built, good-looking guy with a broad, pleasant smile. When John asked him what he did on the outside before he was drafted, he said, "Most of the time, just having a good time." He added, "John, one time I won $27,000 at Hialeah Race Track, but I blew it all on women and booze."

Bill Lawler was also tall, but had a normal build. He had been in the real estate business in the Forest Hills section of Queens before being drafted.

Bill Longran had been a truck driver for the A&P grocery chain before being drafted. He had been married once, but had since divorced. Most of the time, he seemed to have a kind of sad expression on his face.

Prior to the war, Fred Miller had received some military training in the German Army and, boy, could he roll a blanket tight! He was about 5'8" tall and as solid as a rock. He weighed about 165 pounds and spoke with a German accent.

Gene Kowalski was kind of a typical wiseguy from Brooklyn. He thought he knew everything.

One day during basic training, the company participated in a field day in which all of the platoons in the company competed against each other in physical events. The commanding officer from John's platoon, Lieutenant Norocki, who had been an engineer in civilian life, decided that five members of his platoon, the First Platoon, would compete in a tug–of–war against the Second Platoon. John was selected, along with Tom Mullins, Bill Lawler, Bill Longran (who was the oldest), and Fred Miller, the strongest on the team.

The Second Platoon had mostly fellows from the southeastern states, and their commanding officer was Lieutenant Schroeder, who had been a New York City police officer prior to being recalled into active duty. The guys on the other side of the rope outweighed John's squad by hundreds of pounds. There was one guy on the other team nicknamed "Tiny." His feet were so big that the Army didn't have boots to fit him, so he had to wear rubber overshoes. But John was no shrimp himself, standing almost 6 feet tall and weighing about 198 pounds.

As both sides pulled hard, the rope became tight and rigid. No one wanted to give in. Then Lieutenant Schroeder hollered out,

"Come on New York!" With that encouragement, John's group seemed to gather just enough strength to pull the southerners across the line. The other group collapsed and John could understand why.

Basic training was the first time that John ever shot a gun. He and the other recruits were each given a Springfield Model 1903, single-shot, .30-06 caliber rifle. One day during target practice, John was having a lot of fun shooting at the dirt mound in front of the target; he liked to see the dirt fly just like in the movies. As John was lying in the prone position shooting at the dirt, his platoon commander, Lieutenant Norocki, a reserve officer from New Jersey who had been called up to active duty, saw what he was doing and walked over. After kicking John in the heel of his foot, he said, "Mackowski, raise your sights and stop shooting into the dirt. This target practice might just save your life some day."

Another time, when John and his platoon were being trained at attacking the enemy, they were told to fire in a certain direction. On the opposite side of the firing range from where they were standing, there was a small wooden shack. John didn't know who was doing it, but some of the guys began shooting out the windows in the shack. What the men didn't know was that there were range observers in the shack. The range captain was really pissed off by the actions of the recruits and kept the whole group at the range until late in the afternoon. Finally, before the group was marched back to the barracks, the range captain stood before them and angrily asked, "Who's the wise guy?" When no one answered, he repeated, "I said, who was the wise guy that shot at the shack? You could have killed someone!"

When no one answered, he yelled out to the entire group, "Now remember this you sons-of-bitches! You'll wish you'd learned to hit the target, because the United States will be going to war soon and your ass will be in a sling if you can't hit the broad side of a barn! Now put that down somewhere and remember it, you bunch of assholes!"

What the hell is this guy talking about? Who's going to war? John thought. This was the first inkling John had that he might not be home in a year, after all.

John and his buddies were assigned to a typical
Army training barracks, a wooden two-story structure
hastily thrown together to accommodate the increasing
number of new recruits. There were two floors in the
barracks, which was heated by a coal-fired furnace. In
the bathrooms, the toilets were lined up in a row with no
partitions separating them for privacy, and there was a
shower room on one side with about five showerheads.
The bunks were lined up in three rows on each floor. At
one end of the barracks, there was also a small room on
each floor. John's bunk was upstairs. The platoon
sergeant had a room downstairs, and the two corporals
shared a room on the second floor.

One time during boot camp, the three Irishmen,
Mullins, Lawler and Longran, somehow got hold of some
gin and invited John to join them. They had a great time,
and John got drunk. After going to bed for the night to
sleep it off, John had to go to the latrine, which was on
the lower floor. As he headed down the stairs, he tripped
over his own feet and tumbled down the stairs and right
through the screen door. He got up, walked to the latrine,
relieved himself and went back upstairs to his bunk. The
next morning, John's platoon had a unit inspection. As
the men stood in formation in the hot sun, Lieutenant
Norocki and Sergeant Watson, the platoon sergeant,
stopped in front of John whose breath still reeked of
booze. The lieutenant was mad, and the sergeant had a
real stern look on his face.

"Have you shaved today, soldier?" the lieutenant
asked.

"No, Sir!" John replied. (He didn't have much of a
beard then anyway). Turning to Sergeant Watson, the
lieutenant said, "Gig this man and take away his pass for
the weekend."

Fort Belvoir is about 10 or 15 miles from Washington, D.C. John could get a train to New York City and arrive in Penn Station at 34th Street in a couple of hours. From there, he would take the subway to Greenpoint. Because he couldn't get home to Brooklyn on that particular weekend, John asked Bill Longran, who also lived in Brooklyn, to stop by and tell Opal that he was doing OK, and that he would be home the following weekend to sec her. When Longran stopped by to see Opal and give her the message, he wound up getting drunk with her father at the apartment.

John and Sergeant Watson didn't get along from the first day they laid eyes on each other. Sergeant Watson kept butchering the pronunciation of John's last name. During roll calls, when he came to Mackowski, he would always say "Private Moskowski," "Mickawitz," "Moscowitz," but never "Mackowski." It usually took him three or four times before he would pronounce it correctly, and John would never answer until he pronounced his name right. To get even, John would often mispronounce the sergeant's name as well, sometimes calling him "Sergeant Vatson" using a heavy New York City Jewish accent. The other guys in the First Platoon enjoyed this little verbal battle and would often laugh out loud, causing the sergeant to call everyone to attention. John had made an enemy with Sergeant Watson, and it would stay that way for quite some time. Every time there was a crummy detail, Sergeant Watson went to his "shit list" and would usually pick John.

One day, while trying to remove a broken culvert pipe in the road, John and another soldier were each given a shovcl by Sergeant Watson and told to "start shoveling."

"Sergeant, you can't dig this pipe out with a shovel. It's too wet," John said.

"Just do what you're told. If you'd keep your big mouth shut and shovel, you'd be able to do it," Sergeant Watson responded. The two soldiers were dealing with a combination of rock, mud and water, and they were not gaining any ground. Every time they would shovel a load of goo out of the hole, the mud would come sliding back down the sides. Meanwhile, the rest of the guys just stood around laughing and ribbing John and his partner. Some time later, Lieutenant Norocki came by and was really ticked off that the old culvert pipe was still in place.

"Sergeant Watson! Why the hell is that culvert pipe still there?" he yelled. John, who was still shoveling in the ditch, heard what the Lieutenant said and yelled out so that everyone could hear, "If I was a civilian, I would use that winch in front of the truck to pull the pipe out!"

The C.O. heard him and called over, "OK, pull the truck over and use the winch. And we'll see if it works." John wrapped the cable around the culvert pipe, went back to the truck, pushed the lever for the winch and, lo-and-behold, the pipe came out. At that point, the lieutenant told John and the other soldier to come out of the ditch and take a rest while the rest of the group put the new culvert pipe in.

On another occasion, John's platoon was called out to formation. As they stood there, Sergeant Watson kept yakking away. Some of the guys made covert remarks. They would pretend they were coughing, but somewhere during the cough the words "asshole" or "shithead" could be heard. Sergeant Watson never said a word. He just kept on talking. Then, he began to dismiss a few men at a time. The sergeant kept closing the ranks and dismissing the others, but not John. Finally, it got down to John and two others, Gene Kowalski and Benny Cermack, who both also happened to be of Polish descent and from Brooklyn.

First, the sergeant had them march single file, military fashion, around the barracks. After doing this for quite some time, he called out, "At ease!" Then he told one of the corporals, Corporal Delaney, to continue to march them around the barracks. Corporal Delaney wasn't really a bad guy. He was only eighteen, and John was twenty-five at the time.

John, Gene and Benny were getting jeers from their fellow soldiers in the barracks, particularly from Mullins, Lawler and Longran. They were yelling out the windows, "Hey, you guys are out of step!" "You're marching too close to each other!" "Are you guys going out for a couple of beers with us?" They kept yelling, knowing that it would make John mad as hell, and it was working. John was starting to get really ticked off. He wasn't one of the guys who coughed out the words "asshole" and "shithead," but the sergeant was taking it out on him anyway. John decided that he wasn't going to give in to the sergeant so he started counting off as they marched: "Hup, two, three, four; Hup, two, three four; Your left, your left, your left, right, left." It didn't take long before Gene and Benny joined in.

Now the other corporal from the platoon, Corporal Vilamont, came on duty and replaced Corporal Delaney. They kept marching around the barracks with John calling cadence to the tune of "Cozmaline, My Darling." Around eleven o'clock that night, the lights in the barracks went out but the group was still marching. Then Sergeant Watson came out. John started sounding off louder and louder, and the other two "Poles" started laughing. The sergeant issued an order to halt.

Sergeant Watson stood in front of John and said, "Mackowski, if you'll keep quiet, I'll give you an order to execute. If you do it, I'll call it quits." John looked at his two buddies and asked them what they thought. "We're with you," they said. John looked at the sergeant and said, "OK, shoot!"

"Port arms!" the sergeant said, almost sheepishly. The three obeyed and he dismissed them. John and his two buddies ran back to the barracks and up the stairs. As they reached the top, John yelled out so everybody could hear, "I made that skinny bastard say 'uncle'."

Then there was the mess sergeant, a southerner with a heavy drawl who stood about 5'9" and who had a round face. John and his buddies drove him up the wall. Meals were served family-style in deep dishes, with ten men sitting at each table. Soldiers on KP (kitchen police) had to keep filling up the dishes. When the dishes were empty, a soldier would hold them up and the KP's would come over, get the dishes and fill them. It was John's first taste of hominy grits. He thought it was white corn until a fellow soldier told him what it was and that they fed it to pigs.

The mess sergeant hated northerners and would turn to his southern buddies and yell out, so everyone could hear, things like, "Look at these goddamn Yankees eat! They're nothin' but a bunch of goddamned pigs!"

Of course, after the mess sergeant said something like that, one of the northerners on the other side of the mess hall would always yell out something like, "Blow it out your stacking swivel," "Blow it out your barracks bag," or "You rebel asshole!"

That would make the sergeant mad as hell and he would often hold up the mess line so the privates couldn't eat on time. He did this almost every meal, so John and his fellow recruits came up with a system. As they stood at attention at the tables, they would slide the serving dishes to one another, fill up their plates and pass the serving dishes to the next guy. When the mess sergeant finally told them to sit down and eat, there were so many empty plates held high that he would come out from behind the mess line and call them a bunch of pigs. He would go back and forth from one end of the mess hall to the other yelling obscenities at the recruits. When he reached one side of the room, someone would give him the "raspberry" from the other end. Others would make a coughing sound with "asshole" or "shithead" in it, or simply yell out, "Blow it out your ass!" Finally, the sergeant wised up, kept his mouth shut and the problem went away.

John slept in the first bed in the center row, near the stairway on the upper level of the barracks. One night around 9:30, towards the end of boot camp, John was lying in his bunk, half asleep, when he saw a shadow coming up the darkened stairway carrying something. He sat halfway up in bed in order to get a better look, and saw that it was Gene Kowalski with what appeared to be a pail of water. Gene, like John, had no love for Corporal Vilamont, who shared a room with Corporal Delaney, which was located right near John's bunk at the top of the stairs. When Gene saw John sitting up in his bunk, he put his finger to his lips, giving him the sign to be quiet.

John watched as Gene knocked on the door to the room. A voice behind the door said, "Come in!" Gene didn't reply. He just knocked again, this time a little harder. Again, a voice shouted out, "Asshole, I told you to come in!"

Again, Gene ignored the request and knocked again, still harder. Now the door started to open and John could clearly see Corporal Vilamont in the light of the room. His head was still turned towards the inside of his room and he was talking to Corporal Delaney. "I wonder which one of these assholes ...." But before he could finish his sentence, Gene threw the whole pail of water through the opening in the door. The corporal was temporarily stunned and Gene managed to make his escape down the stairs without being identified. John immediately covered himself up with the blanket as he heard the two corporals running down the stairs.

About one minute later, Sergeant Watson and the two corporals came up the stairs and put the lights on. John was still lying in bed with the blanket pulled up over his head, pretending to be asleep. Unfortunately for John, he was laughing so hard under the blanket that his bed was shaking. Corporal Vilamont walked over to John's bed, pulled the blanket off, turned towards the sergeant and said, "I think he did it. Look at him laughing."

John looked directly at Sergeant Watson and said, in a voice that still quaked with laughter in it, "Sarge, he doesn't know what he's talking about. Hell, he's all wet."

Hearing that, most of the recruits on the second floor started laughing. Corporal Vilamont, looking to the sergeant for support, said, "Well, if he didn't do it, he knows who did."

"Do you know who did this?" the sergeant asked.

"No, I don't!" was John's reply. He wasn't about to

be a snitch on his friend Gene. The result was Sergeant Watson had John mop up the whole upper floor of the barracks. Unfortunately for the sergeant, however, he got in trouble with Lieutenant Norocki for keeping the lights on after nine o'clock.

John saw Gene the next day and told him, "I had to mop the whole second floor last night because of you, but don't worry, they still don't know who did it."

"Thanks a lot, Johnny, for not telling, but I just had to do it. I don't like that little snot-nosed son of a bitch."

There was one guy in the barracks whose last name was Jacobs. He had gotten married to avoid the draft, but he had been drafted anyway. He was also the sloppiest guy in the whole platoon, but he somehow managed to always get a weekend pass. Jacobs came from a wealthy Jewish family in New York City, and it was rumored that he was regularly paying the sergeant two bucks for the weekend passes. Jacobs also didn't care for Army food, so when he went on pass, he would often return with his own food, including various kinds of cheeses that he put in his footlocker.

The barracks was becomming infested with ants. One of the guys noticed a trail of ants going in and out of Jacobs' footlocker. Another guy in the barracks, named Soberman, who was also Jewish and from New York City, was really pissed off. He was a rather big guy. He walked over to Jacobs and said, "You're the kind of Jew that makes the world hate us. If you don't get rid of that shit, I'll throw you and your foot locker out the goddamned window." Jacobs quickly got rid of the food.

On another occasion, Lieutenant Norocki did not like the way the platoon was marching in formation, so he told Sergeant Watson that he could determine who would get a weekend pass or not. When John heard that, he knew he was in trouble, because the sergeant hated him. On this particular weekend, Sergeant Watson said he was going to check everyone's rifle to make sure it was properly cleaned before anyone got a pass. John went downstairs with his rifle like everyone else, but when Sergeant Watson looked at it, he said, "This rifle is a disgrace. It's filthy. Go back and clean it right, or you won't be going on pass this weekend."

John made the trip down to see the sergeant several times. Each time he cleaned the rifle again, only to be told that it wasn't clean enough. Meanwhile, Jacobs had paid the sergeant his two bucks and was on his way. An hour and a half had passed and most of the guys were gone, with only John and three others left.

John was starting to really get pissed off. He had already missed several trains to New York City. He went back upstairs and sat down on his bunk thinking that he would never get home for the weekend.

Dave Glazno, who slept one bunk away from John, was lying on his bunk. The guys in the barracks had given Glazno the nickname "goldbrick" because he always seemed to take the easy way out. He was in no hurry for a pass this particular weekend because his wife would be coming down from New York City, as she did most weekends. He was going to meet her in Washington, DC, where they would stay in a hotel. When Monday came, Glazno would probably go on sick call, as he did most Mondays. Seeing the disgust and anger on John's face, Dave Glazno turned to him and said, "Johnny, you're too anxious, and besides that, the sergeant hates your guts. Let me prove something to you. Give me your rifle and I'll show you."

61

John gave Dave his rifle, and he took it down to the sergeant. The sergeant looked at Glazno and said, "That's one of the cleanest rifles I've seen in a long time." With that, Glazno got his pass, came back upstairs and waved it in John's face. John grabbed his rifle back and started to go down the stairs. Glazno stopped him and said, "Wait ten minutes or so, and then bring it down. Watson's just breaking your balls."

John waited about ten minutes, then went downstairs and handed the rifle to the sergeant. Sergeant Watson pulled the bolt back, looked into the barrel and said, "This is more like it, Mackowski." He was smiling. John was fighting back the urge to punch him right in the puss, but he kept his mouth shut, stood at attention and the sergeant finally gave him the weekend pass.

The platoon went out on a 10-mile hike one day, and most of the guys were having a tough time because they were carrying a full knapsack, including shelter half, pegs, bedroll and all sorts of other equipment. Meanwhile, there was this one guy, Private Scorano, from the Flushing section of Queens, who didn't seem to be having any trouble. Scorano was a little guy who only weighed about 118 pounds. He had been in the National Guard and had joined the army after his girlfriend became pregnant. All during the march, Scorano was whistling, singing and wise-cracking. The captain couldn't figure out how he was so full of energy. When they got back to the barracks, Scorano showed the other guys the contents of his pack. It was filled with crumpled newspapers that made his knapsack light as a feather.

There was another guy on the first floor of the barracks, named Daley, who was a real loner. He was always writing letters, but most of the time, the only mail he received was junk mail advertising from companies. Most of the guys in the barracks just left him alone.

Even in the hot, sweaty summer weather of Virginia, Private Daley never took his long underwear off, and no one ever saw him take a shower. Oh, he washed his face and hands, shaved and things like that, but he never took a shower. He was really starting to smell.

One evening, a couple of the guys from downstairs forcibly took Daley into the shower room and gave him a "G.I. shower." He was fully-clothed at the time, and he was screaming and fighting with them all the way. John could hear the yelling and screaming coming from below, so he went down to see what the commotion was all about. As he walked into the shower room, several of the guys were holding Daley under the shower, and he was yelling for help. Finally, the group released him and Daley collapsed on the floor of the shower, crying. He cried all the way back to his bunk. It was a sad sight. Most of the guys in the barracks realized at that point that Daley had some real mental problems. The next day, he was taken from the barracks by one of the sergeants and was never heard from again. Everybody assumed that he had been discharged.

It was now May 27, 1941, and the men had heard on the radio that two U.S. merchant ships had been sunk. President Franklin D. Roosevelt gave a radio address to the nation and declared an unlimited state of national emergency. Roosevelt told the nation that he was extending the U.S. Navy's patrol deep into the eastern Atlantic to ensure the delivery of needed supplies to Britain. It was a significant escalation of an undeclared war on Germany.

After hearing the president's speech, John remembered the range captain's remarks after the recruits were caught shooting at the shack, that the United States would be going to war. After President Roosevelt's announcement, the pace of the training seemed to step up a little bit and some of the guys started to take it more seriously.

Towards the end of basic training, the platoon headed out on a twenty-mile overnight march carrying all of their field equipment. It started raining as the platoon headed out to the field. It is very hot and humid in Virginia in June, and most of the guys were having a lot of trouble on the march. Many had blisters on their feet, and some just dropped from exhaustion. When they finally got to their bivouac area, the men began pitching their pup tents in the rain. They were having a lot of trouble with the tent pegs. Because of a combination of the rain and the clay soil, the pegs kept popping up and the tents kept falling down. Everything was wet. As the men were eating out of their mess kits, the kits quickly filled with rain, turning their dinner into a kind of soup. All in all, it was just a miserable time.

Most of the guys couldn't sleep because of the rain. Then, someone threw a mud ball at another tent and it fell down. So it went all night, with the guys trying to knock each other's tents down with mud balls. One guy even took a crap in front of another tent just to see the occupants step in it when they came out.

At the end of basic training, the whole company was treated to a big dinner prepared by the mess sergeant. He must have been under budget, because they had a steak dinner. The steaks were huge, covering the plates. Although John was a fairly good eater, he had trouble finishing off his steak, but a fellow next to him ate two of these huge steaks. Everyone had a great time.

The training company was now being broken up, and the Army was sending the men to various engineering outfits throughout the country. They were going to combat engineer units like the 36th Combat Engineers, light and heavy pontoon bridge units. John, Gene Kowalski and Morris "Moe" Levine were sent to the 803rd Aviation Engineers in Massachusetts, which was a brand-new outfit.

The three of them were the last to leave the basic training company, and the training barracks were empty when they left. They went by train to Springfield, Massachusetts, where they were picked up and driven to Westover Field in Chicopee Falls, Massachusetts in the back of a deuce-and-a-half truck. Westover Field had been designated as the staging area for the new battalion. After reporting to the 803rd, John was assigned to Company A, 3rd Platoon, 1st Squad. While waiting for supplies and equipment, they were assigned to build a rifle range. Most of the time, John drove a 3/4-ton truck.

The first sergeant of Company A, Clarence Rutz, was about 25 years old, stood about 6 feet 2 inches tall, weighed about 200 pounds and came from Kansas. He told John that he was going to send him to NCO (Non-Commissioned Officer) School. John replied that he didn't want to be an NCO. The first sergeant told him, "Mackowski, the Army thinks you have all the capabilities and leadership skills necessary to be an NCO."

"That may be so," John said, "but I don't want to go."

"Mackowski, you are no longer a civilian; you take orders from us, and you're going," the first sergeant said.

"If you make me an NCO, I'll go AWOL and you'll have to bust me," John replied.

The first sergeant even sent another sergeant, Sergeant Downey, over to speak to John to convince him to go to NCO School. He told John, "You're one of the smartest guy in the company; you should be a Sergeant."

John wasn't convinced. The Army sent him to parts of the NCO School anyway, but John never did get the rating. One day, First Sergeant Rutz asked him, "Why don't you want to be an NCO?"

"I believe that there's a pretty good chance that the United States will be going to war. I can read the handwriting on the wall, and I don't want to tell anyone what to do that might get him hurt or killed. I just want to be responsible for myself. Tell me what to do and I'll do it, but I don't want to give orders to anyone," John said. The first sergeant pretty much left John alone after that, but at times he would put him in charge of other privates.

While at Westover Field, John was assigned to the motor pool as a truck driver. One day, John and a guy named Mario, who resembled the singer, Vic Damone, were in the kitchen peeling potatoes during regular KP duty. John found out that he was also assigned by the first sergeant to KP duty the following Sunday. It made John mad because he wouldn't be able to go home on the weekend to see Opal. He didn't think it was fair. He was already on KP during the week, and he shouldn't be pulling another KP so soon after this one. Just then, First Sergeant Rutz walked into the kitchen to get a cup of coffee. John asked him, "Hey First Sergeant, how come I pulled special KP duty this Sunday when I'm already on KP during the week? I don't mind pulling my fair share of KP, but I'd like to know if my name came up during some sort of regular rotation or not."

"You're on Sunday KP because I need you to drive a truck during the week," The First Sergeant replied.

"Why are you screwing me? Does this have something to do with me not going to NCO school? I'd like to know what the hell am I being punished for?" John asked.

"You're big enough to take it!" the sergeant replied in a very officious voice.

John's temper was boiling. He threw the potato peeler on the floor, looked the first sergeant right in the eye and said, "Yeah, I'm big enough to take it, and I'm also big enough to dish it out! Do you want to try me?"

The sergeant just turned around and walked out of the kitchen. Mario, who had a stunned look on his face, turned to John and asked, "What the hell is the matter with you? Are you crazy? He's the first sergeant."

"I don't give a shit who the hell he is. It's not fair." John eventually got out of the Sunday KP, but he never made it home that weekend because the whole outfit went over to a military reservation in Connecticut for war games. John was taken off the KP list because the motor pool sergeant, Sergeant Richard A. Koerner, convinced the C.O. that he was needed to drive an ambulance.

On July 26, 1941, President Roosevelt issued the order freezing all Japanese assets in the United States. He also announced that he was recalling General MacArthur to active duty. MacArthur would be responsible for mobilizing the Philippine Army with ten million dollars drawn from the president's emergency fund.

The next few weeks passed quickly and before John knew it, it was Labor Day weekend of 1941. At around the same time, the newspapers were filled with the information that 60,000 Japanese soldiers had landed in Indochina. Some of the units were assigned to security details and were not allowed to leave the post. The FBI had alerted all military bases to step up security, and John's outfit, which was considered a combat unit, was one of the units that had to stay on the base to provide additional security. John managed to call Opal, and she came up to the base to visit him, but because of the long trip, she could only stay and visit with him for about 45 minutes.

On September 23rd, the men were told that they would be going overseas. All passes were canceled and rumor had it that they would be going to the Philippines. John and Gene Kowalski talked about the unit going overseas. They knew that this weekend would be their last chance to go home for quite a while, so they decided to go AWOL on Saturday morning.

In order to get off of the base, he and Gene walked through the woods to avoid the MP's, eventually coming out on the main road outside the base. The two young soldiers were picked up by a local radio announcer, who was on his way to New York City to visit his girlfriend. He told them that he would play the new Army Air Corps song ("Off we go into the wide blue yonder ...,") for them on his show on Monday. Thanks to this unknown announcer, John and Gene arrived in Greenpoint on Saturday afternoon around 4 o'clock.

They split up. John went directly to Opal's apartment and then visited with his family, while Gene went to visit his family. John went out with Opal on

Saturday night and said goodbye to her on Sunday afternoon. He and Gene hooked up again in Brooklyn, took the train to Springfield and arrived back at Westover Field on Sunday evening just before roll call. They checked in with the company clerk, Private Gilbert Soifer, and found out that they were never marked down for being AWOL. It was almost as if the sergeants knew what the men would be in for, and just looked the other way.

A few days later, John and his fellow soldiers loaded their equipment on a military train and headed through the Housatonic Tunnel and out across the country, stopping now and then for food and supplies. One stop was at a tomato cannery in Indiana where many of the guys bought tomatoes. Another stop was in a rural area of New Mexico where small children, who looked like Mexicans or American Indians, ran down a hill and stood alongside the railroad tracks. John didn't know where they came from, but they sure looked hungry and poor.

He didn't know who started it, but the soldiers on the train began giving the children handouts. The kids, who were dressed in ragged clothes, were very excited and ran up and down a small hillside. John saw one little girl, maybe about six years old, who was barefoot and wearing a well-worn dress. She had very long black hair and the biggest, brightest brown eyes. All John had to his name were a nickel and two oranges that were left over from his lunch. He gave them to the girl. She smiled at him and then ran up the hill, shouting as if she had found a million dollars.

During the long train trip, John pulled KP duty and it was one of the dirtiest details he was ever on. The kitchen for the troop train was located in a converted baggage car towards the rear of the train. The mess sergeant was Sergeant Max Hurwitz, who had been a chef in one of the famous Jewish hotels in the Catskills prior to being drafted. He assigned John to give out sliced bread during one of the meals. He told John that he had just enough bread to go around. "I don't care who you're serving, they only get two slices."

One of the sergeants from his company, Sergeant Forest E. Wooley, who was only about nineteen years old, had a reputation as a "chow hound." He stopped in front of John. Per instructions from Sergeant Hurwitz, John gave him two slices of bread, one of which was the heel.

"Hey, what's this? I'm a sergeant, and sergeants don't get any heels. Give me a regular slice of bread!" Sergeant Wooley yelled at John.

"I don't care who you are. My instructions are to give every man two slices of bread, and that's what you got. So keep moving – you're holding up the line!" John told him. The sergeant refused to move until some others waiting on line began to yell, "What's the holdup?" "Come on, keep the line moving!"

Two days later, the troop train arrived at the Presidio in San Francisco. John never had a chance to leave the base. His group stayed there only one night, and then the thousand officers and enlisted men boarded the Tasker H. Bliss transport ship (formerly a Dollar Line ship) and headed out of San Francisco Bay, past the Farallon Islands and towards Hawaii. There was another transport ship, the Willard H. Holbrook, which was accompanying the Tasker H. Bliss to form a two-ship convoy.

Soon after they left San Francisco Bay, they hit rough waters and John got seasick. He tried to eat, but he was too sick. He couldn't hold anything down, so he stayed below for the first few days. It took him a couple of days to finally get his sea legs.

There wasn't much to do on the ship between meals. The men passed the time "topside" watching sharks, flying fish and dolphins swim near the ship. They played cards and just "shot-the-shit" to pass the time. A couple of nights, movies were shown on the deck.

Probably the most annoying part of the entire voyage was Sergeant Wooley playing the song "You Are My Sunshine" over and over again on the ship's loud speakers. It was driving the men crazy, and they joked about throwing Sergeant Wooley and his records overboard. Luckily, the men were also able to listen to Mel Allen calling out the plays from the 1941 World Series games between the New York Yankees and the Brooklyn Dodgers.

The ship docked for a short time in Honolulu. The weather was warm and tropical and the ocean water was clean and clear. It had a beautiful bluish-green color which made it very inviting, but unfortunately for the soldiers on board, they were not allowed to leave the ship.

As the two transports dropped anchor in Honolulu, the men crowded on deck to see the island. It was more beautiful than any picture in any magazine that they had ever seen. They could see Waikiki Beach, Diamond Head (an old volcano) and the palm tree-fringed white-sand beach with large waves rolling onto the shore. There were lush green mountains beyond the city which were dotted with pineapple plantations and beautiful homes.

One of the soldiers aboard the Tasker H. Bliss, Private Joe Gozzo, wanted to see Hawaii and somehow during their short stay managed to jump ship, even though the dock was crowded with MP's in white helmets. He was caught after the convoy left Honolulu, and was sent to the Philippines on the next transport, the U.S.S. Coolidge.

About two days out of Hawaii, the two transport ships were joined by a new 10,000-ton Navy cruiser, the U.S.S. Chester, which had been named after the city in Pennsylvania. Rumors were flying all over the ship about the United States going to war with Japan. John was having a difference of opinion with one of the soldiers, Marco Caputo, who came from upstate New York.

"All of us guys on this ship are going to be fighting the Japanese," John told Marco.

"You're full of shit," Marco replied. As they were arguing back and forth, Marco called over to one of the sailors, "Hey goomba, tell this old Polack that he is wrong about us going to war with the Japanese."

The sailor looked at John and said, "Look, kid, when I walk down the street of any Jap city, them slope heads make way for me. There's not going to be any war," the sailor boasted.

"Then tell me, asshole: What the hell is that cruiser doing out there?" John asked. The sailor did not answer and walked away. The other guys on the deck, who were listening to the conversation, said nothing. Even if they didn't know for sure that we were going to war, they all had that thought in the back of their minds. They just didn't talk about it. Many just stared out at the calm sea or at the great albatrosses that flew along the ship every day.

The convoy was delayed for a day or two in Guam, because the Holbrook had boiler trouble, but it wasn't long before they were on their way again. As the ships moved closer to the Philippines, they began practicing blackouts, running without lights. It was a great chance to see beautiful ocean sunsets, or flying fish, porpoises and phosphorescent fish swimming in the black water at night. On one occasion, the ship's captain called out over the PA system, "If you guys want to see something, take a look on the starboard side and see the sharks."

There were no radio transmissions or wireless messages sent out anymore, except for emergencies. They were in dangerous waters, close to the Mariana and Caroline Islands which now belonged to the Japanese. During the daytime, the sun shined down brightly on the men. Many had either acquired a tan or had been somewhat sunburned. The air was getting very humid and heavy. Luckily, the breeze from the moving ship helped a little. The ships passed the International Date Line on Tuesday evening around midnight, so there was no Wednesday for the men that week. They went straight from Tuesday to Thursday.

The third week of October, almost three weeks since they left Honolulu, someone yelled out that he could see some smoke on the horizon. It wasn't long before they could see the top of Mount Mayon, with whiffs of smoke rising out of the still active volcano. The deep green beauty of the many islands was mesmerizing to those aboard the ships, particularly for those who were viewing the Philippines for the first time. The ships passed slowly through the San Bernardino Straits passing numerous small islands and then headed northward. They could see sandy beaches, large plantations and small fishing villages with tiny bamboo huts on stilts. Men, women and children were waving to the soldiers from the small villages, as were the fishermen on their outrigger boats with brightly-colored sails. There were fishing nets drying in the sun along the shore. You could see people sitting on or walking alongside large water buffalo, children playing games at the water's edge, and even some people swimming in the ocean.

The ships first headed northwest into the China Sea, eventually turning northeast past the small island of Corregidor on the left, and into Manila Bay. John could see large snakes swimming alongside the ship as they came closer and closer to the docks. It reminded him of the story of Frank Buck, of "Bring 'em Back Alive" fame, who had caught the world's largest python in the Philippines.

The Tasker H. Bliss was now slowing down and heading towards the pier. Ever so gingerly, the ship slipped into a berth at Pier 7 and the engines stopped. John and his fellow travelers were now officially in the Philippines. The dock was a flurry of activity, with Navy personnel unloading vehicles, equipment and other cargo from the ships. As the men looked out over the sides and waited to disembark from the ships, they realized how comfortable it had been when the ships had been moving and creating a breeze. It was now so hot and humid that most of the GI's uniforms were wet from perspiration. The smell of cocoa, banana, tobacco and other sweet smells combined with the smells of the sea.

The men could see the old battlements on the ancient wall near the Old Spanish enclave. There appeared to be some very elegant buildings in the vicinity of the breakwater, like the palace of the U.S. High Commissioner on Dewey Blvd., located across the open field from the Manila Hotel. John's first impression of the Philippines was that the country was very beautiful, with palm trees all over the place. It looked more beautiful then anything he had ever seen in the National Geographic magazine. To him, the Philippines looked like paradise.

Chapter 3

ARRIVAL IN THE PHILIPPINES
October 1941

After the Tasker H. Bliss docked at Pier 7, which was also called the "Million Dollar Pier," John and his fellow soldiers got their first close-up look at the native Filipinos. They were very dark, in stark contrast to the lily-white American soldiers and sailors who were scrambling around the docks and coming off the ships. The Filipinos on the dock reminded John of pictures he had seen in National Geographic magazine. The men were wearing short pants, with shirts worn outside of their pants. Most of the women were wearing long skirts and blouses, but there were a few women who were bare-breasted. A lot of the guys on the ship were hanging over the railing, whistling and yelling catcalls at the bare breasted women. It wasn't long before the order came down for the soldiers to pick up all of their gear, head down the gangplank and stand in formation on the dock

As the group was standing around waiting for further orders, John saw a "regular army" man from the

31st Infantry Regiment standing on the dock. He walked over to him. "How do you guys like the Filipino women? They look pretty dark, don't they?" he asked.

The Infantryman's answer was short and to the point. "Let me tell you this, soldier: the longer you stay here in the Philippines, the lighter they get."

Just then, before he could ask any more questions, John saw a convoy of trucks heading onto the dock. Within minutes, the whole battalion boarded the open "deuce-and-a-half" trucks and headed north for the two-hour ride to Clark Field. As the convoy headed for the entrance of Clark Field, John could see a large number of older planes lined up in the fields and near the runways.

The next day, after all of the equipment was off-loaded from the ships, John and the other truck drivers from the 803rd Engineers were driven back to Pier 7 in Manila to pick up their own trucks, which were now loaded with heavy construction equipment and other supplies. For the first few days at Clark Field, the individual companies in the battalion would line up in formation after breakfast, and individual squads, or in some cases just one or two men, would be assigned to specific work details around the air base. After a few days, however, the battalion was split up, with each of the companies going to different places. The Headquarters Company stayed at Clark Field. Company A, John's company, went to Camp O'Donnell, which was located between Iba to the east and Cabanataun to the west. Camp O'Donnell consisted of nothing more than a large number of hastily-built wood and bamboo barracks with thatched roofs made of cogan grass and with side walls of sawali or nipa in woven sections. Many of the framed panels were hinged and could be propped open to catch any slight breeze that might blow by. Company B went to a place called Del Carmen, which is south of Clark Field, and Company C went to Nichols Field, near Manila. All of the companies were assigned either to build airstrips or to maintain them.

As soon as Company A arrived at Camp O'Donnell, the enlisted personnel were assigned to six-man tents. The sergeant placed John in charge of the five other guys in his tent. They were Privates Morton Karp, Rudolph "Rudy" Kiena, Ken Stull, Frank Windle and one other guy.

Private Windle had been an electrician in civilian life, and he was always trying to catch butterflies to send back to his sister in the states. He never did get a chance to ship them out because the ants always got them. They stripped everything off the cardboard.

That first night, while John was writing a letter home, he saw a large dark-green snake coming across the floor and heading in his direction. He yelled out, and Kenny Stull killed it with his entrenching tool.

John was assigned to the motor pool working for Sergeant Metras Trefel. One day, towards the end of October 1941, John was assigned to drive Sergeant Desel Davisson, the Company A supply sergeant, down to Clark Field to pick up the laundry. On the way back, John saw a soldier standing on the side of the road near one of Company A's trucks, which had its hood up. As they got closer, John recognized the soldier as Private Frank DiPasquale, originally from Brooklyn, whose nickname was "banana nose" for obvious reasons. John pulled his truck to the side of the road, parked behind the disabled truck, got out and asked, "Hey, Banana Nose, what's wrong?"

"I don't know. The engine quit on me. Could you give me a tow back to the motor pool?" DiPasquale asked.

"It's OK with me, but I got to ask Sergeant Davisson." John walked back to his truck and yelled out to the Sergeant, "Hey, Sarge, can we tow Banana Nose back to the motor pool? There's something wrong with his truck."

The supply sergeant, in a very officious voice, yelled back at John, "Let the motor pool come and get him. That's their job. I have to get the laundry back to O'Donnell."

John turned to Banana Nose and told him, "You heard the sergeant. I can't do it. But don't worry: when I get back to the camp, I'll stop by the motor pool and make sure that they send someone out for you."

As they started to drive away, DiPasquale looked at John and the sergeant and said, "Yeah, thanks for nuthin'!" When John got back to Camp O'Donnell, he stopped by the motor pool, told one of the mechanics about the truck that had broken down and gave him the location.

The next morning, as soon as John arrived for duty at the motor pool, Sergeant Trefel came up to him and started to shout, "Hey Mackowski, I don't want anybody in my motor pool who refuses to help another driver!"

"What are you talking about, Sarge?" John asked.

"I'm talking about what you did to DiPasquale yesterday!"

"Wait a minute, Sarge," John said. "It wasn't my decision. Sergeant Davisson wouldn't let me tow Banana Nose back. I stopped in the motor pool as soon as I got back to camp, and told the mechanics that he had broken down and where he was."

"I don't give a shit what you told to who!" the sergeant yelled back. "We got a rule in this motor pool.

79

We help the other drivers no matter what, so you're outta here. Go back to your company."

The motor pool sergeant turned and walked away. As he did, John started walking behind him trying to reason with him. "Hey, sergeant, that's not fair. I wanted to help Banana Nose, but Sergeant Davisson wouldn't let me," John explained.

"I told you, I don't give a shit. Go see the first sergeant. I'm sure he'll find something else for you to do. All I know is you ain't driving one of my goddamned trucks no more."

John was not given a chance to explain any further, and Banana Nose didn't say anything about the supply sergeant not allowing John to help. That same morning, John was back in line duty, working mainly as a laborer. It seems that from that day on, John and another guy from Company A, Private Andy King, would always be in trouble.

The guys in Company A came from all walks of life. There were all sorts of tradesmen, a few lawyers, and even one or two Wall Street stock exchange workers. One of the former stock exchange workers, Walter Flowers, who was very neat, had a slim build, wore glasses and was a very hard worker, surprised John one day. As they were working on a detail, Walt Flowers spoke to John in very good Polish. John was stunned and just smiled. Then John asked Walter, "How come you speak such good Polish?"

"I learned it at home. My parents came from Poland," he said.

"But you don't have a Polish name!" John replied.

"I changed my name in order to get a job on Wall Street. If I had kept my Polish name, I never would have gotten a job." Every once in a while after that, John and Walter would speak to each other in Polish.

One of the guys from Company A, Rudolph Pfeifer, kept pretty much to himself and was rather distant from the other guys. He had attended Syracuse University and had been a star on the football team. When he was drafted, his dream of being a big-time football star faded. He was a big fellow with huge feet. One night, not long after he was promoted to the rank of corporal, he returned to camp firing his .45 caliber pistol in the air. No one was hit, but the next morning John heard that Pfeifer had said he fired his gun because there were snakes all around him. He was relieved of his pistol, taken to the military hospital at Clark Field and never returned to the company.

Another guy in the company, Private John Parsons, was always bitching about everything. His favorite saying was "The Army's chicken shit." He was about thirty years old, skinny and a heavy drinker, but he was an expert with all sorts of heavy equipment. His wife had divorced him just before he was drafted, and he was very bitter. Parsons had opened the porthole on the transport ship during rough weather while en route to the Philippines. When the seawater came pouring in, Parsons yelled to everybody that the ship was sinking. They all had a good laugh over it.

Another guy, Joe Minder, from North Creek in upstate New York, was also bitching all the time. Paul Boback, from Pennsylvania, always had a wad of chewing tobacco in his mouth. John would often watch as Boback bitched about one thing or another and then spit out a mouthful of tobacco juice. Boback hung out with a guy named Joe Vater from Pittsburgh.

There was a corporal in another platoon who was very young, and whom everyone seemed to dislike. He always had a sour-puss and talked down to the men, most of whom were quite a bit older than himself. One sergeant John liked was a Native American, Sergeant Grubbs Anderson, whom everyone called "Chief." Sergeant Anderson was a heavy drinker who often got busted back to corporal for short periods of time.

The NCO's in Company A were mostly "regular army" men, although some draftees eventually became corporals and sergeants. One of John's sergeants was a draftee. Every time there was extra work to do, Sergeant Steve Kruchowsky would come and get John. On one of these occasions, John asked him, "Hey, Sarge, how come when there's some extra duty you always come and get me?"

"When I come and get you it's because Captain Zbikowski ordered it, not because I'm breaking your balls," the sergeant replied.

"What does he have against me?" John asked.

"I don't know. You'll have to take it up with him." John was only a private. He thought it best to just keep his mouth shut and hope the captain would lighten up on him.

In early November 1941, John received two newspaper clippings from Opal. One of the articles quoted President Roosevelt saying, "no selectees would be sent to foreign soil." The other article quoted General Marshall with saying practically the same thing. Opal had written in ink above the article, "Why are you there?"

John started to make comments about the articles to his buddies. He showed the clippings to them and they, too, were pretty mad. Morton Karp asked him,

"What are you going to do about the newspaper clippings?"

"I don't know," John told them. But then he thought: These guys have a right to know what the hell is going on. If the President says we're not supposed to be here, then why the hell are we here? He didn't tell anyone what he was going to do, but later that afternoon he tacked the articles up on Company A's bulletin board. Later that evening, John was ordered to go see Captain Zbikowski, the company commander, in his tent. As soon as John walked into the tent, the captain looked at him and said, "Mackowski, did you post those newspaper clippings on the board?"

"Yes, Sir, I'm the one who did it," John replied.

"Why did you do it?"

"I thought I'd let the fellas know what's going on back in the States."

"You're not authorized to put anything on that board. Do you understand that, Mackowski?" the Captain asked.

"Yes, Sir, but I didn't know you had a rat in this outfit," John replied.

The captain, who had been a teacher in civilian life, was starting to get angry. He said, "What do you mean you didn't know I had a rat in the company?"

"In Brooklyn, we call people who tell on other people 'rats'." John replied. Mocking the captain's background as a school teacher, John added, "To you sir, they are probably called tattle tales."

The captain was now mad as hell and called the first sergeant over. "First Sergeant, see to it that Mackowski gets extra guard duty for the next two weeks! Dismissed!" John and the First Sergeant left.

John's first assignment was to guard a building where lumber, cement and other building materials were stored. With John on this first night of guard duty was a young private from the South named Travis Flowers. He wore glasses, had a boyish face and was normally very quiet. There were animals of all kinds walking through the surrounding jungle and making all sorts of strange sounds. It almost seemed like there were a lot more noises in the jungle at night than in the daytime. Flowers kept talking and talking, right from the beginning of their shift. And he kept repeating himself: "Do you think there's any Japs out there? Do you think we're going to war? Did you hear that? What will we do if we're attacked? "What do you want to do when you get back home?"

John was trying to catch a few winks since it was customary for one guard to sleep while the other was awake. But every time John tried to doze off for twenty minutes or so, Flowers started to talk to him, asking some of the same questions again. As the night wore on, Flowers was driving John crazy with his incessant talking. John thought, Why doesn't this guy just shut up? Why does he keep talking and talking? I got to get some sleep. So at last, John turned towards Travis and told him in a loud whisper, "For Christ sakes, Travis, won't you please shut the hell up so I can catch a little sleep!"

After telling him to keep quiet, John felt bad and thought, This young kid must really be scared. That's probably why he keeps talking and talking. Hell, I'm from the city and never camped out in my life. I'm the one who should be scared, not him.

In any case, Flowers kept quiet long enough so that John could catch a couple of winks, and no material was stolen that night.

On another night, John was on guard duty right near the Company A bivouac area when he observed Sergeant Forrest Wooley talking to a Filipino man. A short time later, he saw Wooley, another soldier and a Filipino woman entering a tent. It was obvious that he was having a sexual rendezvous with her, probably for the going rate of fifty centavos. After a while, the sergeant came out and looked a little startled when he saw John standing near the tent, like a little boy who had been caught with his hand in the cookie jar.

"Ah, ah, hey, John. What's happening?" he said in a halting voice.

"Oh, nothing. It's been pretty quiet so far, except for you and your lady friend," John replied, knowing that he had the sergeant dead to rights. It was an unusual predicament for a private to be in. Here was a sergeant that didn't like him (and, of course, the feelings were mutual), and now the sergeant would have to be nice to him, at least for the next few minutes.

There was a short silence as the two just stood there and looked at each other, then Sergeant Wooley broke the ice, "Go ahead, John. If you want to have her, I'll cover for you."

John thought, He's just asking me because he knows I got him good. But he just looked at the sergeant and said, "You don't have to worry about me, Sarge. I ain't seen nothing." Then John turned and walked away from the sergeant and continued on his rounds.

85

While at Camp O'Donnell, there was a private in the company named Carl Biggs who hailed from Tennessee. He told everyone he was half-Indian, and decided to wear a Mohican haircut. He had about two inches of hair running from the front to the rear of his head, the rest having been shaved clean. The whole company got quite a charge out of it. The captain didn't like it, however, and he ordered Biggs to shave the rest of his head to get rid of it.

Another private named Andy King could best be described as a "lost soul." His wife, a nurse back in the States, had divorced him, and shortly thereafter he was drafted into the Army. He was kind of a fun-loving guy who seemed to like John, whom he called "Chee-Chee." Why he called him "Chee-Chee", John would never know. On one occasion, Andy bought a monkey at a shop in one of the local barrios and brought it back to camp with him. Another time, he brought an eight-foot python back to camp. He had it wrapped around his shoulders and was laughing. Luckily, the captain ordered him to get rid of the creatures each time he brought them to the camp. John felt kind of sorry for the guy. It seemed that he was looking for friendship, but most of the other guys in the company thought he was just a clown.

On a pass day, John and Andy King decided to take a walk from Camp O'Donnell to the local barrio, which was only about a mile away. About three-quarters of the way there, they came upon a small roadside stand where a woman was selling soda and snacks. They each bought a Coca-Cola to drink. While they were drinking their sodas, the woman kept staring at John. She was about twenty-five years old and not bad looking. John and Andy were just passing the time looking at the three or four small children who were running around the nipa shack.

Then John saw the woman in the upper level of the shack. She was looking at him and making a hissing sound. All John knew was that, back in Brooklyn, when someone hissed at you, you had probably screwed up or said something you weren't supposed to say. What the hell is she doing? Maybe she's just nuts, he thought. He turned to Andy and said, "What's wrong with her? Why is she making that hissing sound?"

"She wants to have sex with you, you dope," Andy said.

"What do you mean she wants to have sex with me? What the hell are you talking about?"

Andy was prodding John to go upstairs with her, "Go ahead Chee-Chee. Go up. She's waiting for you."

"Nah, I don't think so," John said, but Andy kept pushing.

"Come on, let's take a crack at her."

Just then one of the little boys, who couldn't have been more than 9 or 10 years old, told John in broken English, "My aunt would like to have "puk-puk" with you."

"Go ahead. If you go, I'll go," Andy said, but John was taken aback by this "kid pimp" and refused the invitation.

"No thanks, we don't have the time. We've got to get back to the base," John told the little boy. Andy wouldn't go in either, because John wouldn't. As the two men left, Andy kept looking at John, making the "pluck, pluck, pluck" sounds of a chicken all the way back to camp.

Prostitution is no stranger to any military installation, especially when thousands of men are stationed far away from home and their wives and girlfriends - and the Philippines were no different. There was a path leading from Camp O'Donnell to the main road where a local Filipino man would regularly "pimp" a couple of native women, charging the soldiers a peso for a quick fling. It was becoming a problem because many of the soldiers were coming down with a variety of sexually transmitted diseases. Captain Zbikowski eventually found out about it and told the first sergeant to post guards on the path with orders to remove anyone from the area. One night, John was assigned to guard duty with Rudolph Kiena, one of his tent mates, who came from Pennsylvania and whose nickname was "the Dutchman." As was the practice, John and the Dutchman would alternate staying awake, one hour on and one hour off.

While John was resting and the Dutchman was standing guard, Andy decided he would sneak up on John and scare the hell out of him. It was a very dark night, cloudy and with no stars. The only sounds were from small animals moving about in the dark and from bats flying overhead. Unfortunately for Andy, the Dutchman was standing guard and not John. Andy jumped out of the jungle and almost scared the Dutchman to death. The Dutchman said, "What the hell's the matter with you? You almost scared the living shit out of me, you dumb asshole! Now get the hell out of here, fast."

Andy could see that his efforts were in vain as he still had not awakened John, who was sleeping against a tree. "I'm not going anywhere until I talk to John," Andy said, and he just stood there and refused to move.

"I'm not telling you again, asshole. Get the hell out of here," the Dutchman said in an angry tone. When

Andy still didn't move, without saying another word, the Dutchman stuck him in the butt with his bayonet. Andy let out a scream, yelling at the Dutchman,

"You stabbed me, you Kraut bastard. Look at the blood!" The noise and commotion woke John up and he came running over.

"What the hell is going on?"

"The son-of-a-bitch stabbed me in the ass with his bayonet," Andy yelled.

"Get the fuck out of here or I'll stick you in the ass again, you dumb asshole," The Dutchman yelled back.

"I'll get you for this, you son-of-a-bitch," Andy yelled to the Dutchman. Then he turned around and left quickly to get some medical help for his bleeding butt. About fifteen or twenty minutes later, First Sergeant Rutz walked up to the guard post, walked over to John and said, "Hey, Mackowski, you know that Private King had no business here."

"Yeah, I know," John replied.

"He got stuck in the ass because he refused to leave. The Dutchman did nothing wrong," Sergeant Rutz explained.

"I know. He came up here to scare the hell out of me and, boy, he didn't expect to get stuck in the ass," John said. With that, the first sergeant left.

"What the hell was that all about?" the Dutchman asked.

"Oh, the sergeant knows I'm friends with Andy, and I guess he doesn't want me to get in a fight with you." John and Rudy laughed about the incident all night until they finished their tour.

A few days later, on a Saturday afternoon after mail call, the guys were sitting around the tent when the

Dutchman showed everybody a letter he had received from his wife. He was sitting on the side of his cot and had a big smile on his face.

"What are you smiling at?" John asked the Dutchman, but he received no answer.

"It looks like you got some good news from home. Did you?" John asked.

"Yeah, I guess my wife still loves me," the Dutchman answered. "How can you be so sure?" one of the other guys yelled out. The Dutchman smiled, turned to the other guys in the tent and slowly reached into the envelope.

"What you got in there, gold?" someone yelled.

"Better than gold," the Dutchman responded, grinning from ear to ear as he pulled some strands of pubic hair from the envelope and ran them over his moustache. No one made any more comments. They all just smiled at each other.

One day, Corporal Louie Jay had been given the job of securing a location for a latrine and building the structure with some local Filipino laborers. He was having an awful time trying to make himself understood by the four Filipino civilians who were getting paid to help. Unfortunately, the corporal had chosen a place by the river where the soil was very sandy, and every time the men dug into the sandy soil, the sides would collapse back into the hole.

First Sergeant Rutz saw what was going on and, knowing that the Corporal was in over his head, he came over to John, who was working nearby, and said, "John, do me a favor. Go over to where they're building the new latrine and help out the corporal. He's having some trouble." John walked over to the site and tried to talk to the Filipino laborers, but it was obvious that they didn't understand him, either. So he decided to work alongside them and show them how to shore up the sides of the hole using wooden boards and some 2x4's. After lunch, the first sergeant came by to check on the progress. When he saw that it was almost finished, he turned to John and said, "Mackowski, you did a goddamned good job, a goddamned good job."

John was assigned to another job in which a sergeant was having trouble getting some Filipino laborers to work hard enough. It seems that some of the Filipino civilians were either loafing on the job or stealing building material from one of the construction sites. John was given the assignment of checking on every Filipino on the job site. He had help from a interpreter named Charlie Lee, a Chinese-American who had been born in California, but who had come to the Philippines to attend the San Tomas College because it was cheaper than colleges in the United States. Lee was a nice guy.

Part of the job involved supervising the shipping of lumber and cement to the airstrip that the company was building near Camp O'Donnell. One day, Lieutenant Walter Farrell, drove up to where John was standing and said, "Private Mackowski, you have to get these workers to work a little harder. They are not working hard enough, and we need more cement at the airstrip." Then he drove off.

Geeze, what the hell does he want from me? Here I am with six Filipinos, each one carrying a bolo knife strapped to his side, and he wants me to lean on them to make them work harder, John thought. All John had with him was his old, World War I issue Springfield rifle. The odds were stacked against him, and he was getting madder by the minute. He thought, What the hell does he want from me? I'm only a private. Why doesn't he send a corporal or sergeant down here to boss these guys around?

As he watched the six Filipinos struggling to push a barrel of cement up two wooden planks and onto the truck, he got so pissed off that he handed his rifle to the interpreter and told the laborers in English, "Move away from the goddamned barrel and I'll show you how to do it!" John got behind one of the 450-pound barrels, which were made of tin and had wooden lids on either end, and started pushing as hard as he could. He was so angry that he somehow managed to push the barrel up the ramp and onto the truck. Although he was a little winded, John turned to the interpreter and said, "Tell them if one man can move a barrel onto the truck by himself, the six of them can load the truck up a lot faster."

Later in the afternoon, Lieutenant Farrell came by again, but this time he told John, "Jesus, John, slow down a little. Stop sending the cement up to the airstrip. We don't need any more."

"Pardon me, Sir?" John said.

"Slow down a little here."

"Why, Sir?" John asked.

"Because there are several other trucks up there now that still have not been unloaded and things are backing up."

"OK, if you say so," John replied. Then he, the six Filipino workers and the interpreter took a break for awhile.

On another occasion, while driving a truck, John saw an unusual sight. A beautiful young Filipino woman was taking a shower outside of her house. She had on a thin skirt, but no top. She had a pleasant face and a rather well-built body. When he saw her, he thought, What the hell is this woman doing? Taking a shower outside the house? He slowed the truck down to get a better look.

The woman quickly realized that John was looking at her, but the fact that he was staring at her didn't seem to bother her. In fact, she turned around, faced him straight on and their eyes met. She kept pouring water over her head from a small pot. Then she lathered up with soap. And then she would repeat the cycle. The water ran down a slit trench and into the jungle. John just smiled at her, and she looked at him as if to say, "What the hell are you looking at?" But she didn't move. She just stood there staring at John. John smiled back as he put his truck in gear and drove away, thinking, Man, I've never seen anything like this before. The guys back home in Greenpoint will never believe me if I tell them. Wow! This is some country!

It was now November, and the soldiers were working six days a week to get the airstrip built. One evening, a group of eight or ten men from Company A received permission to go to Clark Field, which was about forty miles southeast of O'Donnell. As the group got on a truck, First Sergeant Rutz came over and told them, "I want every man in this truck back here by ten o'clock. Behave yourselves and don't get into any trouble." Then he looked to see if there was an NCO in the truck, but there was not. He then looked over to John and said, "Mackowski, you're in charge of the group. Make sure they all come back by ten." With that, they left for Clark Field.

John and a couple of guys went to the PX and the rest of the guys went to the barrio looking for sex. By 9:00 PM, all but two had returned to the truck on time. John located the two stragglers in about fifteen minutes and brought them back to the truck. While sitting in the back of the deuce-and-a-half on the way back to the camp, he told them both, "If you two sons-of-bitches get me into trouble with the first sergeant, I'll beat the crap out of both of you." Luckily for them, the group arrived back at Camp O'Donnell by the 10 o'clock deadline.

The next day, the first sergeant came to John and said, "I see you got the men back here on time," but John didn't answer him. He learned from one of the other guys in his company sometime later that one of the two fellows who were late was gay. The guy never came out on work details. He was assigned as the company clerk. The regular company clerk, Gil Soifer, had to return to the squad. The men guessed that they kept the gay soldier inside so they could keep an eye on him.

On December 1, 1941, the men of Company A were given an overnight pass and were allowed to go to Camp John Hays for a little rest and relaxation. After arriving at Camp Hays by truck, the men decided to hike up the mountain to Baquio City. To get there, they had to walk up steep mountain roads. John would never forget one particular section; it was called "the Zig-Zag trail." They would walk a short distance and turn sharply in one direction, then walk a short distance and turn sharply the other way.

On the way, the group stopped at a place overlooking the mountains. They could see a beautiful waterfall in the distance, called the Bridal Falls. John remembered hearing about the Bridal Falls in a geography class about the Philippines when he was attending John Erickson Junior High School in Brooklyn. He also remembered the teacher telling the class about the legend that if you stood before the falls and made a wish, it would usually come true. While looking at the falls, he yelled, "I hope I get the hell out of here, real quick!"

Little did he know what the future had in store for him. Later that day, they arrived in Baquio City where the air temperature was cooler than down below. In fact, it was quite pleasant.

As the men were walking around the city, they heard a voice with an American accent call out, "You boys just come from the U.S.?" The question came from a Protestant minister who was doing missionary work in the city. He was glad to see some fellow Americans and reminisce about the United States, even if it was just for a short time. While in the city, John bought two mahogany bookends that had very beautiful hand carvings of water buffaloes on them.

On the way back down the mountain, John was standing in the back of the open truck looking forward over the cab when an insect flew into his mouth. He didn't think much of it, and by early evening he and the others had arrived back at the camp.

The next morning, John was sick with a 103 fever. An ambulance took him to the Fort Stotsenberg hospital. The doctors thought that he might have malaria, so he was kept at the hospital for two days. During the stay, he was sitting up in bed reading the English-language newspaper called the Manila Bulletin. A nurse came by, pulled the paper away from him and said, "Do you know you have a fever of 103 degrees? You should be resting and not reading."

He smiled and told her, "This is the first paper that I have read in months. I want to know what's happening. I have a right to know if we're going to war." She gave him back the paper, and he read about how the situation between Japan and the United States was deteriorating. Shortly thereafter, he went back to his company.

Chapter 4

AT WAR WITH JAPAN
December 1941

It was just after breakfast on Monday morning, December 8, 1941, and the members of Company A were standing in formation. Usually, one of the sergeants handled roll call and made the daily assignments, but today was different. The captain was coming out to make an announcement.

As was his usual practice when making an announcement, Captain Zbikowski came out of the CP (command post) tent. This time, however, he was not only accompanied by the Lieutenant, but also by several of the NCO's, most of whom wore grim looks on their faces. The Captain looked different too — a little pale, even a little nervous, like someone who was going to deliver some very unpleasant news. As he slowly walked over to the company formation, the guys started talking amongst themselves.

"Hey, look at his face."

"He looks pretty serious."

"It can't be good news."

"He looks like he just shit in his pants."

"Something's got to be wrong."

A moment later, the captain stood in front of the group and addressed the men. "Men, we are now at war with the Japanese. From now on, give your best for your country, for God and for your family. God bless you, and good luck to you all." He said nothing else. He made no mention of why the United States was at war with the Japanese. He just turned and headed back towards his tent.

What the hell did the Japanese do that we're at war with them? John wondered. With that, the first sergeant stood in front of the group. "OK guys. You heard the old man. We're at war with the Japs. We got a lot of work to do this morning. We're gonna break camp and move out."

"Hey, Sarge! What happened?" one of the guys yelled out.

"The Japs bombed Pearl Harbor. That's all I know," the first sergeant replied. He looked up and down the ranks for a few seconds and then yelled, "Alright men, fall out and break camp on the double."

A short time later, as the men of Company A were knocking down tents and stacking cots, mattresses and the pillows in a pile, they could hear the distant drone of airplanes. The noise became louder and louder until two waves of Japanese Mitsubishi twin-engine bombers flew directly over Company A's area. They turned and headed south in the direction of Clark Field, where John had seen large numbers of B-17 bombers and fighter planes neatly lined up on the airfield on the first day he arrived in the Philippines. I hope those planes are not still on the ground, he thought. They'll be picked off like sitting ducks.

A few minutes later, the deep rumbling sounds of the bombing could be heard, then plumes of thick black smoke could be seen coming from the direction of Clark Field. Most of the men just stood there for a few moments watching the billowing black smoke in silence. One guy yelled out, "This is it. The Japs are bombing the shit out of Clark Field. We're probably next!"

It was at that moment that John fully realized the United States was actually at war with the Japanese. It was no longer some abstract possibility to be talked about with the other guys while sitting in your tent at night. It was real, and the men were scared. They weren't talking much, but you could see the fear in their faces.

John began to think about the possibilities. I wonder if I'll ever get out of here. I hope I get to see my family and Opal again. Maybe they'll get us the hell out of here. He was brought back to reality when he heard one of the sergeants call out to the soldiers: "Stop daydreaming, soldiers! We've got work to do. We've got to get out of here as quick as we can, so let's get back to work."

The men of Company A quickly finished breaking camp. They covered all the supplies that were stacked up and left them where they stood in the center of what was their bivouac area. The company moved out, heading south towards a place called Del Carmen.

Early that evening, as it was starting to get dark, Sergeant Kruchowski and John were riding in a jeep patrolling the roads around their company area when they ran across a lieutenant and four enlisted men from another unit. The lieutenant ordered John and the sergeant to pull over.

"What's up, Lieutenant?" the sergeant asked.

"Some local natives reported that a bomb fell in the area, but it didn't explode, and I need you two guys to help us try and find it." After walking up the hill and looking around in the dense underbrush for about twenty minutes, John and the sergeant located the "bomb." It was an empty external fuel tank that had apparently fallen off one of the Japanese bombers. John looked at it with the aid of a flashlight and saw a highly-polished chrome plate on the fuel tank with the inscription, "Made by the L.C. Smith Company, Brooklyn, N.Y."

"This is just great," John told the sergeant. "The goddamn Japs are going to be bombing us with shit that's made in America. If I ever get back to Brooklyn, I'm going to look up the son-of-a-bitch that made this freaking thing and knock him right on his ass."

The next day, December 9th, John was assigned to drive Lieutenant Farrell in a jeep from Del Carmen to Camp O'Donnell to pick up a civilian engineer. On the way, they noticed a group of Filipino soldiers and an American Army lieutenant standing by the side of the road looking up towards the sky. The American lieutenant was waving his right arm indicating that he wanted them to pull over. As soon as he stopped the jeep and turned off the engine, he could hear that same deafening noise that the Japanese bombers had made the day before when they flew over Company A en route to Clark Field.

John grabbed his rifle and jumped off the jeep, followed by Lieutenant Farrell. They ran into the jungle and hid behind a huge Mango tree. Several Japanese bombers flew directly overhead heading in the general direction of Del Carmen. After the bombers passed over, the two men walked back to the jeep and stood beside it for a moment looking towards the sky.

At that point, the lieutenant that had been with the Filipino soldiers came over to Lieutenant Farrell and John and said, "Didn't you guys see them Jap bombers?"

"No, Sir. If it wasn't for you, I guess we would have just kept going," John replied, without saluting.

John then turned to Lieutenant Farrell and said, "Do you think that those Jap bombers are heading towards our company?'

"I don't know, John!" the lieutenant said.

"Gee, I hope not," John added.

"I guess we'll find out when we get back," Lieutenant Farrell said as they both got back in the jeep. The two then continued on their way to Camp O'Donnell. When they arrived, they saw a man in his 60's dressed in civilian clothes standing next to one of the buildings.

"Are you the engineer we're supposed to pick up and take back to Del Carmen?" the lieutenant asked.

"Yeah, that's me. But I'm not going up there."

"Why not?" Lieutenant Farrell asked. The lieutenant was kind of surprised that they had come so far to pick this guy up and he had no intention of going with them.

"I'm getting the hell out of the Philippines. The only place I'm going is home. I'd have to be crazy to stay here," the man said.

John and the lieutenant understood. After all, the engineer was still a civilian; he didn't have to go. John hadn't envied many people in his life up to this point, but now he envied this engineer who would soon be on his way home. Lieutenant Farrell and John left the engineer standing where they had found him. They went over to the mess hall and had something to eat, gassed up the jeep and headed back to Del Carmen.

When they arrived back at their company later that afternoon, they found out that the bombers they had seen earlier in the day had, in fact, dropped some of their load in the vicinity of the Company A camp at Del Carmen. A lot of the guys were shook up, but no one was hurt.

The very next day, December 10th, three Japanese bombers appeared in the skies. As before, the men of Company A could hear the bombers coming long before they could see them. They must be after something big, like Manila or Corregidor. John thought, as he and the others watched them approach. But as the planes were directly overhead, the unmistakable screeching sound of falling bombs could be heard, and everyone ran for cover. John dove into a nearby muddy pool next to a palm tree and partially submerged his face, swallowing some muddy water in the process. As he lay in the small pool of water, he could feel the concussions from the bombs as they hit the ground. The force actually raised him out of the water several times. When the bombing finally ended and he pulled himself up, he was choking on the muddy water and gasping for air.

One of the guys in the company came over to him and asked, "Mackowski, are you hit? Are you alright?"

"Yeah, I guess so. There's nothing broken."

John made a promise to himself right then and there that whenever he heard the planes coming, he would not hesitate to find a place to take cover. As he looked around, he saw that a nearby nipa shack had suffered a direct hit. He ran over and helped pull the bodies of a Filipino man, his wife and his two little children from the ruins. All four were killed when their house collapsed on top of them.

On Friday, December 12th, the men were told that the Japanese forces had made their first landings in the Philippines, at Aparri on the northern coast of Luzon. Most of the Japanese bombings were now taking place in other parts of the Philippines, although an occasional Jap bomber would fly overhead and drop some of its payload in the vicinity of Company A.

John and his fellow foot soldiers were not privy to a lot of information about what was going on, but it appeared to them — or at least so they believed — that the American and Filipino troops were holding their own against the Japanese. In reality, the Japanese forces were slowly driving southward. Then, two pieces of bad news came down. They learned that the British forces on Hong Kong surrendered to the Japanese on December 19th and a few days later, on Monday, December 22nd, word came down that the Japanese 14th Army had come ashore in the Philippines, at Lingayen Gulf.

That same day, while the company was at GauGau, Captain Zbikowski ordered the mess sergeant to prepare a Christmas dinner with turkey and all the trimmings. The men of Company A didn't know it at the time, but that turkey dinner was to be their last cooked meal for quite some time.

The next day, General MacArthur ordered the withdrawal of all U.S. military personnel and Filipino soldiers to the Bataan peninsula. Bataan is twenty-five miles long, and twenty miles wide where it connects to the island of Luzon. Mountains occupy its middle, running like a spine from the north to the southern tip. Like most of the Philippines, it is carpeted with thick jungle on the mountain slopes and farmland on the eastern coastal plain. There was nothing but a dirt road running from the southern part to central Bataan, which then crosses over to the eastern part. Company A moved to the southwest side of Bataan in the area of kilometer 201 near Marveles, and the men faced out towards the South China Sea. The other three companies from the battalion were detailed to the east side of Bataan.

Sometime around January 7th, 1942, word came down that small groups of Japanese soldiers had begun landing on the west side of the Bataan peninsula. It appeared that they were not yet ready to risk a full frontal assault against the American and Filipino forces. The men from Company A had some short-wave radios, which they listened to constantly. There was Tokyo Rose playing songs like "Don't Fence Me In" and telling the men, "Hey, Joe, why are you fighting us when your wives are shacking up with other guys back home? Why stay here and fight for people you don't even know?"

The men were told to go to the command post to see the captain. When they arrived at the tent, the captain told them that everyone in the company was to take out GI insurance for ten thousand dollars. He said, "Men, we don't know what is going to happen to us. The least we can do is take care of our families by leaving something for them." John decided to take out the insurance, even though the payment of $6.60 per month was pretty stiff considering a private was only getting thirty dollars a month, and a PFC thirty-six dollars a month. John thought, The captain is making sure we all take out insurance. I guess he thinks we're all gonna get killed.

On January 8, 1942, realizing that it wasn't looking too good for the Americans and Filipinos, John decided to bury many of his possessions in the area. If

I'm gonna get captured or killed, I'll be damned if I'm gonna let the Japs get any of my stuff, he thought. So, he buried all of his worldly possessions, which consisted of a camera, the two mahogany bookends and several other small items.

Rumors were running rampant throughout the company that aid was on its way and that a relief convoy of seven ships was coming from the States. There were also rumors that some Japanese troops who were reported to have landed earlier on Bataan were now in the area near Company A. Unfortunately, the latter rumors turned out to be factual. After doing work on a road detail that day, John pulled guard duty at the base of their camp at 2:00 AM. The soldier John relieved told him, "Keep low and shoot anything that moves, because it could be a Jap." It was pitch black and John couldn't see much, but he finished his guard duty shift without event.

The next day, the company was assembled and the captain told them, "Men, some Japs have landed nearby and we've been assigned to go into the jungle and take care of them. We've been assigned to assist the 45th Infantry. The place that Company A will search is called Agloma Point." They were told that some remnants of the Filipino army and Filipino constabulary were also in the area and would be assisting.

John's Springfield rifle was taken away from him and he was temporarily issued a Browning Automatic Rifle, commonly called a BAR. The only time John had ever fired a rifle was back in basic training at Fort Belvoir, and he had never fired a BAR at all. His entire unit, Company A, 803rd Air Corps Engineers, was not trained for combat duty. But there he was, holding a BAR, with no instruction on how to use it, and heading into the jungle in search of Japanese soldiers. Just before they left, a guy in the company looked at John's BAR, pointed to the weapon and said, "Hey, Johnny! Do you know how to use that thing?"

"I think so!" John replied.

"I hope you know that your weapon is on full-automatic," he said.

Of course, John didn't know what the hell he was doing. He quickly switched it back to single shot.

"That's better, Johnny. I feel a lot safer now," the other guy said as they headed into the jungle.

As the company of soldiers began to fan out, John's squad moved out on the left flank. They all moved with caution, and yes, most of them were scared stiff. Just a few months ago they were accountants, truck drivers, electricians and construction workers, and now they were heading out into the jungle to fight one of the crack army units from the 14th Imperial Japanese Army. They knew that the Japanese soldiers were very well trained, and that Company A was neither trained nor prepared for this kind of assignment.

As the unit moved deeper into the thick foliage of the jungle, they started to receive sniper fire from camouflaged Japanese soldiers, many of whom were up in the big Banyan trees where they couldn't be seen. When the gunfire started, John didn't know who was firing at whom. An occasional "pop-pop" could be heard, followed by a barrage of gunfire. Everyone was looking up at the trees. The Banyan trees reminded John of rockets; the roots came out from the tree like the fins on a rocket.

Someone called out, "There's a sniper firing from up in one of the trees!" And the tree was sprayed with bullets from a Browning, water-cooled, .30 caliber machine gun from World War I. In fact, most of the equipment the men were issued had been first issued in World War I. John threw several grenades, as did other guys in the squad, but none of them went off.

"How the hell do they expect us to fight these Jap bastards if our friggen' grenades don't go off!" one guy yelled out.

In order to bolster Company A's lines, a company from the 45th Filipino Scouts joined up with them. John thought, These guys look like they really know what they're doing. The Scouts were physically small but they looked pretty fierce.

As they continued their search for snipers, John could see Private Joe Minda pinned down ahead of him, taking shelter behind a big tree. As John watched, he could hear shots being fired and could see the bullets making their marks on the tree. John was afraid to tell Joe to move because he feared that if Joe made the wrong move, he would fall into the sniper's sights. Finally, Joe Minda dropped to the ground, moved away from the tree and took cover behind a rock, out of sight of the sniper. The American soldiers quickly learned to move very quietly. They were told that the Jap snipers wore sneaker-like shoes that were split around the big toe, which gave them a better foothold when they climbed up trees. The snipers also strapped themselves to the trunk of trees or limbs after they got into position. Many times, the men could hear the Japanese soldiers yelling out in broken English, "Go home, Joe!"

At one point, a call came from the central part of the company line. "We need a BAR man! One of the Jap snipers has us pinned down!" John was the only guy in the vicinity who had a BAR. He looked over to Sergeant Steve Kruchowsky, who looked back at John, but he didn't say anything.

"What do you want me to do, Steve!" John yelled over to the sergeant, but he didn't answer.

"I'll go up there, OK?" But the sergeant still didn't answer. John made up his mind and decided to go up anyway. When he got to the location, Sergeant Carl Hendricks, who the men called "Babyface," yelled, "Them lousy, Jap bastard snipers are hitting my men! If you see one of them, shoot! Let him have it!"

The Japanese snipers were very clever. They would let the GI's walk past them, and then they would shoot them in the back. As John waited for a sign of movement, the sun broke through the trees and he caught a glimpse of an empty cartridge falling from a tree about 10 feet away. He put his BAR on full automatic and sprayed the crotch of the tree. As he did, some of the other snipers began firing on John. One shot was very high and to John's left. Another was way out to the right and made a puff of dust as it hit the ground. John looked over to Sergeant Hendricks and said, "I'm getting the hell out of here and going back to my squad!"

"No you're not! You're staying right here!" the Sergeant replied.

"Sarge, I don't give a shit what you say! I came here on my own, and I'm going back on my own to my own squad!"

"You're staying, and that's an order!"

John pointed his BAR in the Sergeants direction and said, "I'm going back to my squad where I came from."

As he left, blood started to run down from the crotch of the tree. The bullets from his BAR had found their mark.

Just as John got back to his squad, the Japanese opened up with heavy firing. Private Joe Fritzel looked over at John and said, "Jeez, John. You looked like you were really enjoying yourself. You kept smiling while you were firing away at them Jap bastards."

"Maybe I was smiling, but I was scared as hell," John said. Just then, another one of the guys in the squad, Teddy Darby, threw a grenade. They all ducked, but it didn't explode.

"How do they expect us to fight these bastards when all they give us is shit equipment!" Darby yelled out.

"Some more of that great World War I stuff," John added.

During the course of the firefight, John fired his BAR so much that it became very hot and then jammed. This is just great, he thought. I'm in the middle of a freaking war and my freaking gun doesn't work. He looked over to Steve Kruchowsky and said, "Hey, Sarge, my goddamned gun's overheated or something. It doesn't work."

"Give it to me. I'll see if I can fix it." John crawled over and gave the BAR to the sergeant.

Just then, John heard someone calling out for a medic. "Medic, Medic, I've been hit!" He looked up and saw Sergeant Delbert Moore coming through the jungle calling for help. Moore had been shot in the arm and was bleeding very badly.

Sergeant Kruchowsky called out, "Somebody help him!" No one answered. "Can someone take him to the first aid station?" the Sergeant yelled out, but no one moved.

John called out to Sergeant Kruchowsky, "I don't have any gun anyway, so I'll take him out!" He made his way over to the wounded sergeant. He took the sergeant's 45 caliber pistol, put the sergeant's good arm over his shoulder and helped him back to the command post, which was three-quarters of a mile away and where the temporary aid station was set up. When he got there, he could see wounded soldiers lying all over the ground, with doctors and medics feverishly working on some of them.

One of the medical officers, Captain Herbert Coons, seeing John carefully place Sergeant Moore down on the ground, ordered him to assist with loading wounded soldiers into the ambulance. The driver yelled to Captain Coons, "I need someone to ride with me." John was ordered to go with the ambulance to the base hospital at Marveles. There was no room for John in the passenger side of the ambulance so, with his newly-acquired, Colt .45 caliber pistol in his hand, John rode on the fender of the ambulance all the way back to the medical unit tent in blackout conditions.

The next day, John was back at Agloma Point. He was next to another Army Air Corps private who was using a shotgun to shoot at the snipers. Of course, shotguns were not issued, so John asked him, "Where the hell did you get that shotgun?"

"I bought it at one of the barrios," the man replied. "It might be illegal to use a shotgun, but with the shitty equipment they're issuing us, we've got to use something against them sneaky Jap bastards who don't play fair, either." John's company was at Agloma Point for more than two weeks. The fighting went on day and night. The Americans did not get much to eat, nor was there much water available. At night, the Japanese soldiers would use tracers to draw fire on themselves. Then, when the Americans would fire back, other Japanese soldiers would shoot at the American positions. Eventually, the men received orders not to fire back under those circumstances.

One guy drank some water that was used to cool off the machine gun and got very sick. One soldier wet his pants, another defecated in his pants, and one guy kept calling for his mother in Italian after he was shot. Another guy, from Kansas, Private Elmer Yockum, got so mad that his machine gun jammed that he stood up and yelled, "Come on out, you bastards, and fight like a man!" He threw his helmet down on the ground, and as he did, he received a bullet in the center of his forehead. He fell down and died instantly.

The Americans and Filipinos kept pushing the Japanese down the steep hill to the South China Sea where huge mortars from Fort Hughes were finishing them off. The men of the U.S. Navy, with their makeshift ships, shot the hell out of the Japanese landing barges, which kept reinforcements from reaching the Japanese invaders at Agloma Point.

In their first encounter with the Japanese, Company A of the 803rd Engineers lost 7 to 10 dead and 15 wounded. Among those killed were Privates James Kenny, Robert Reh, Ray Goldback, Paul Gellert, Elmer Yockum, and Privates Jacobellis and Sullivan. A corporal who nobody liked had been shot in the shoulder, apparently by friendly fire.

Shortly after the Battle of the Points, Company A moved to the area around Marveles. While at this location, John's squad was on patrol when they saw General Douglas MacArthur pass by in his olive-drab

Packard passenger car en route north to visit the soldiers on the front lines to boost their morale. When he passed by the men of Company A, one of the guys yelled out:

"Hey! Who was that?"

"It's Dugout Doug!" One of the other guys yelled out.

"Who?"

"Dugout Doug. That's MacArthur's nickname. He got it because he's always in the tunnel on Corregidor."

"Who gives a shit."

"So what!" someone else said, and everyone laughed.

The news from the regular AM radios was not very encouraging. The men heard that on February 15th, 1942, General Arthur E. Percival, the governor of Singapore, had signed an unconditional surrender, and 70,000 British troops had been taken prisoner by the Japanese. The Japanese were now dropping leaflets on the troops on Bataan. Some of the leaflets landed in the vicinity of John's squad. They read: "MacArthur is comfortable in the tunnel. What about you? and "With this leaflet, you can go to any Japanese soldier and be treated as a guest."

Things were starting to get real bad on Bataan. Japanese bombers were flying overhead unchallenged, dropping bombs at will. The Japanese were pretty much in control of the air and the sea. Rations were starting to get low, and the men were cut down to only one or two meals a day, usually rice with either canned salmon or tuna. They were told to wear their dress khaki uniforms because their blue fatigues stood out in the jungle. The officers were told to wear their insignia bars on the tips of their collars, because if they wore them on their shoulders, the enemy could easily spot them and pick them off. It hadn't rained since war was declared, so at least the men could sleep outside without fear of getting wet.

The men in Company A were assigned to various work details while on the west side of Bataan. One group was making a concrete fortification for an eight-inch naval gun. When the emplacement was finally completed, the men were told that some artillerymen from Corregidor would be arriving to fire it. When John saw a Japanese cruiser repeatedly pass by the American positions real slow, he yelled out to anyone who could hear him, "Why doesn't someone fire that goddamned gun and sink that Jap ship?" But the gun never fired. For some reason, they were not being allowed to fire at the cruiser. John thought, There's probably no one here who knows how to fire the fucking thing, anyway.

One day, while Company A was working on a bridge, John noticed a Filipino Army colonel driving by in a jeep. When he saw the Americans, he stopped the jeep and got out to talk to them. In very good English, he said, "That's pretty hard work, eh soldiers?" John and the other men were all dripping wet with sweat at the time. "I just wanted to stop to personally thank you for working so hard to defend my country." Then, after shaking hands with all of the men, he left as quickly as he had come.

On several occasions, the men observed an Army 'deuce-and-a-half' truck which seemed to be loaded with cases of foodstuffs pass by their location. There was always a Filipino soldier armed with a machine gun sitting on top of the cargo. Food was getting scarce, and when people are hungry, they take chances. The soldiers were lucky if they received one meal a day now.

John knew that there was a sharp turn on Westside Road near a steep hill that the truck had to climb, and he knew that the driver would have to slow down and downshift in order to get up the hill. One day, when John saw the truck coming, he went into the jungle and got into position alongside of the road. As the truck driver downshifted, the truck slowly passed the place where John was hiding. In an instant, John jumped out of the jungle, reached into the back of the truck and yanked a whole case off the truck. As it fell off, John ran across the road and into the jungle on the other side. He ducked for cover, fearing that the Filipino soldier would shoot at him, but he didn't.

After the sound of the truck died away, John went back onto the road and opened the case. It contained twenty-four cans of salmon. He went back to his position and gave two cans to every man in his squad, keeping two for himself, but he was bothered by the fact that he had stolen it. Why did I steal the food? What if the food was supposed to go to someone who was worse off than me on the front lines? He thought.

A few days later, the company went to Marveles and John went to see the Catholic chaplain in an open field. He confessed to the priest, "I stole a case of salmon from a truck that was passing by my company's location."

"What did you do with it?" the priest asked him.

"I took it back and gave it to the men in my squad."

The priest smiled and said, "Don't worry, Private Mackowski. God will forgive you for what you did." For penance, he told John to say three "Our Fathers" and three "Hail Mary's." John was a religious person, so it made him feel much better that he told the priest what he had done and the priest told him not to worry about it.

General MacArthur tried to rally the troops with an Order of the Day back on January 15th. His Order told the defenders of the Philippines that help was on the way from the United States. "Thousands of troops and hundreds of planes are being dispatched," he told them, and added that a determined defense would defeat the enemy attack. When the thousands of troops and hundreds of planes failed to arrive, a mood of fatal resignation seeped along the front-line foxholes. By day, the American and Filipino defenders were assaulted by relentless enemy air and ground attacks; by night, constant taunts from loudspeakers and the din of firecrackers made rest impossible.

Chapter 5

ON TO CORREGIDOR
February 1942

The situation was starting to get real bad on Bataan. There were constant aerial bombings and artillery barrages, day and night. In late February 1942, Company A, which was still in the vicinity of Marveles, was ordered to go to Fort Mills on Corregidor.

Corregidor is a small island, about three and a half miles long and one and a half miles wide, its shape somewhat resembling a tadpole. It is located about two miles off the tip of Bataan, in Manila Bay. It was considered an island fortress.

It was very dark the night the men of Company A boarded a couple of barges and left the southern part of Bataan for Corregidor. As they were crossing Manila Bay, the batteries of Fort Hughes were firing towards the eastside of Bataan. Every round that went overhead sounded like a freight train going by. That sound was followed by a ringing sound made by the casing as it came off the artillery shell.

The barges docked at a small wharf at a place called Bottomside, near the low point of the island of Corregidor. The men got out and stood in a sort of informal formation on the dock for a few minutes before being split into several groups. This would be the last time that Company A would have a company formation, and the last time that John would see most of the guys. John's squad, which included Sergeant Steve Kruchowsky, Privates Bailey, King, DiPasquale, Snitzer and four or five others, was sent out to a place called Monkey Point. The other squads were sent to places like Middleside (where General MacArthur and his wife were staying) and Topside, and one of the squads stayed in the vicinity of Bottomside.

John's job from the first day he arrived on Corregidor was to drive one of the two deuce-and-a-half dump trucks that was still in running condition. He was assigned to haul dirt and gravel from Bottomside to the Kindley Field airstrip. The airstrip had a short runway that was only good for small planes like the Stearman Biplane, which had a top speed of about 90 miles per hour.

Every day at about 9 o'clock in the morning, Japanese artillery would open up on Corregidor from Cavite. About an hour later, three or four Japanese bombers would fly over and drop their payloads on the island's defenders. In the afternoon, usually around two or three o'clock, the Japanese bombers would return and drop some more bombs. This was the same standard operational procedure that the Japanese were using on Bataan just before Company A had left for Corregidor.

The men were being fed about twice a day, but rations were becoming very low. They were not able to

take baths, and they were still wearing the same
uniforms they had been wearing at the battle of Agloma
Point. They were dirty and smelly. Wherever John went,
he always took with him his Springfield Model 1903, .30-
06 caliber rifle, with six extra 5-round clips and some
additional ammunition.

The Navy was in the process of constructing a
tunnel, which they called the Queens Tunnel. This
tunnel was supposed to connect to the main tunnel,
Malinta Tunnel. Pvt. Frank DiPasquale, who was
operating a derrick-bucket loader, told John that the
Navy was looking for some help and needed a dump
truck. John and a Navy truck driver named Freddie were
pretty much operating on their own and would go
wherever they were needed.

A few days after, John was drinking a canteen cup
of hot chocolate, which was really hot, when he noticed a
Filipino Air Force staff sergeant sitting opposite him on
the road to Monkey Point. John had gotten the hot
chocolate from some Navy men for doing them a favor.
John thought that the Filipino sergeant looked very
hungry, so he said, "Here, have some."

"No, Sir, I cannot take it. It's all yours," the
sergeant replied.

"Ah, take it," John insisted. Up until that time, no
one had ever called John "Sir." The Filipino was a staff
sergeant, and John was just a private. That was the
beginning of a very short friendship between a kid from
Brooklyn and a young man from Batangas Province.

The next day, a naval ensign by the last name of
Beale asked John to do some work at the Navy tunnel
site, which he did. In return for his help, the young
ensign gave John a can of Libby's peaches. He split the

peaches with the Filipino staff sergeant, whom John called Leo because he couldn't pronounce his last name. Leo thanked John for the peaches and told him that when the war was over, he would like John to meet his wife and child.

Because John drove a truck, Ensign Beale asked John on several occasions to do him some favors, which he always did. One day, the ensign told John that a submarine would be coming to Corregidor for one last mission. John asked him how he knew this, and Beale told him, "Every time a ship is scheduled to come in, my C.O. tells me to put together a loading party." He told John that he could get a letter out for him, and it would probably be the last submarine leaving the island. He told John, further, to use as the return address the 14th Naval District, c/o Post Master, San Francisco, California. Ensign Beale had an arrangement with an Army intelligence officer by which they could get the letters out without them being censored. It seemed that one hand washed the other, so to speak.

In any case, this was the last letter that John would be able to send out to Opal before he would be captured. (He later found out that Opal became quite confused by this letter because of the return address. She thought John was on some sort of special assignment, because she knew he was in the 803rd Engineers. She actually wrote to the postmaster in San Francisco trying to find out where John was).

On March 11, 1942, some of the guys in the squad were listening to a short-wave radio when they heard that General MacArthur had left the Philippines in a PT boat during the night and was heading for Australia. They had heard the roar of PT boat engines during the night, and now they knew what it was about. There were mixed reactions to MacArthur leaving.

"Shit! It don't look too good for us if old Mac is getting his ass out of here," one of the guys said. Some of the men were very bitter that they had been left behind.

"He'll be nice and safe in Australia," one guy said.

"Who the hell are we? Nobodies!" another said.

"I guess we're in for it now," a third man said. Shortly thereafter, an Air Force enlisted man tried to get off Corregidor by flying one of the old Stearman Bi-planes off the island. Rumor had it that he was shot down by the Japanese somewhere near the island of Cebu. After that, there was no one leaving Corregidor.

A rumor was still going around that some kind of aid was coming from the States. There was talk about B-17's and/or a convoy of American ships coming with relief supplies and men. It seemed to make the men feel better to believe that the aid was coming and that they would soon be out of danger. John thought, If some kind of aid is supposed to be coming, then why the hell did MacArthur take off for Australia? But even though the men talked about the aid coming, in their hearts most of them knew that help wasn't on the way. Still, it gave them a glimmer of hope.

John's squad was now bivouacked in the vicinity of the Kindley Airstrip. One day, a flight of Japanese bombers flew over and dropped most of their loads on Topside and Bottomside. It was a good day for the defenders of Corregidor because the American gunners shot three of them out of the sky. Every time one of the big bombers fell from the sky in flames, a roar of cheers could be heard from one end of the island to the other.

Sergeant Kruchowski and his men had ringside seats for one air battle. A flight of four P-40's and a Stearman Bi-plane were on a mission to photograph gun sites around Cavite. The Stearman, nicknamed "the Blue Goose," was piloted by a Filipino captain. Its wings were painted a bright orange/yellow, and the rest of the plane was painted a dark blue.

At the time, there were still some Navy ships on the east side of Corregidor. The U.S.S. Mindanao (a gunboat that had been stationed in China), the U.S.S. Finch (a minesweeper) and the U.S.S. Pidgeon were positioned in the waters between Bataan and Corregidor. John and his fellow squad members had a great view of them looking out from a high spot on Monkey Point.

The men couldn't see where, or if the Blue Goose had landed on this particular day, but they did see a P-40 land at Cabcaben on Bataan, where Company B of the 803rd had built an airstrip. There was another P-40 circling the airfield waiting to land, but unfortunately for him, there was a Japanese fighter right on his tail. The P-40 pilot took some evasive action and dove down towards the Navy ships with the Japanese fighter right behind him. When the P-40 passed by the ships, the Navy gunners opened up on the Japanese plane. John and his buddies knew it was hit because they could see smoke coming out of the plane, and it looked like the pilot was having a tough time controlling it. It limped back towards Manila in a kind of zig-zag pattern. The P-40 landed safely a few minutes later.

On April 8th, the squad was working at night at the airstrip. John was taking a short nap in the cab of his truck as it was being loaded with dirt. All of a sudden, he could feel the truck shaking. He shouted to Frank

DiPasquale, who was using a bucket loader to load the truck, "Hey Frank, stop shaking the goddamned truck!"

"What the hell are you talking about? We're not shaking the truck," DiPasquale yelled back.

"Then who the hell is?" John replied.

Suddenly, they all felt a tremor underneath their feet. Several of the guys yelled out that it was an earthquake. They looked over at Bataan and saw balls of fire and could hear explosion after explosion. It was obvious that either the Japs were hitting some ammo dumps or the Americans were blowing them up so they wouldn't fall into the hands of the Japanese. It was a fireworks display that put fear into every man on Corregidor.

One fellow in the squad summed up the feelings of all the men when he whispered to John, "We're next." No one spoke much after that. At some point in the early morning hours of April 9th, it became very quiet, and the men learned that our troops on Bataan had surrendered to the Japanese.

A few days later, John was driving his truck away from the airstrip after dumping a load of gravel off when a group of Japanese bombers appeared in the sky. John couldn't hear the drone of the bombers because the truck he was driving made so much noise. The engine was "pinging" like hell because they were mixing gas with kerosene and anything else that would burn just to make them run. As John was driving down the road, a soldier came out of his foxhole and pointed to the sky. John stopped the truck and turned the engine off. Then he heard the Japanese planes. It seemed like they were directly overhead. The bombers were coming from the east this time; they usually came from the north.

He grabbed his rifle and ran for the nearest foxhole. Something told him to get out of there, so he jumped up and ran towards the edge of the cliff and hung on to the roots of a tree. He could hear the whistling of bombs as they were raining down around him. Bombs were exploding, and he was bouncing up and down. The concussion from one bomb took his breath away for awhile. When the bombing finally stopped, John was in a state of shock. He called out as loud as he could, but no one answered. There was an eerie silence. The truck he had just left was a total wreck and was burning. The foxhole he had first jumped into was now a huge hole, having suffered a direct hit. You could fit two trucks in it. John began to shake. He called out again, but no one answered, so he decided to walk down to the Malinta Tunnel. When he arrived at the tunnel, he met a couple of guys from Company A, including Andy King.

"Hey, John. Are you OK?" Andy asked him.

"Yeah, I guess so!" was John's reply.

"Jeez, you look like shit!"

"I don't know what happened, but I know I almost got killed in that last bombing at Monkey Point. I think I'll stay here, outside of the tunnel for the rest of the night."

"Good idea!" Andy said.

John saw that Andy was walking with a cane, so he asked him, "What happened to you?"

"I sprained my ankle." Then Andy limped away. That was the last time he saw Andy King.

John and a couple of other guys from Company A saw a sergeant and asked him what they should do. He said he didn't know, so they decided to stay outside of the tunnel for the night. There didn't seem to be anyone in charge, or at least anyone who knew what they should do. But John and his buddies didn't want to be known as having "tunnelitis," which was the term used for those soldiers who hung around the vicinity of the tunnel because they thought it was safer, so the next morning, the group headed back to Monkey Point to join their unit.

On another occasion, shortly after a Japanese bombing attack, a Japanese photo reconnaissance plane, which the Americans called "Photo Joe," was flying overhead taking pictures to survey the damage caused by their bombers. American gunners managed to hit it with anti-aircraft fire. Photo Joe was sent back towards Manila, smoking and flying in a zig-zag pattern as the Americans and Filipinos on the ground whooped it up. When you're on the ropes, even the smallest victories can't be overlooked.

During one particularly heavy shelling, a piece of shrapnel evidently cut a lanyard on the rope that was holding the American flag up on its flagpole. As the flag started to come down, two soldiers ran to catch it before it hit the ground. Those two unknown men repaired the damaged lanyard and hoisted the flag back up the flagpole. They did all this while the Japanese were shelling their positions.

The foliage was starting to disappear on the island as a result of the constant shelling, and there were really no trees or other shelters to hide behind anymore. The island fortress was quickly becoming barren.

Every day after the fall of Bataan, it was worth your life just to go to the bathroom. The men had to race from their foxholes, do their business and run back as fast as hell. The shelling was continuous, 24 hours a day, and the Japanese bombers came over twice a day, morning and afternoon. At night, the Japanese would have a battery of guns "fire at will" just to keep the Americans and Filipinos awake. It seemed to be working. Most of the defenders were nervous wrecks, and many were becoming shell-shocked. John didn't know what was keeping him and the other men going.

One day, from his foxhole at Monkey Point, John saw a flight of American B-17 bombers come up from the south, from the direction of Mindanao Island. The next day, the men learned that the B-17's had bombed Clark Field, which was now being used by the Japanese, and had taken them by surprise. It was a morale booster for the Americans, but the shelling and bombing continued.

The Japanese began lining up their artillery at Cabcaben and facing them out towards Corregidor. Their biggest piece was a 240mm cannon. On the Emperor's birthday, April 29th, the Japanese threw everything but the kitchen sink at the American and Filipino troops. Two large ammo dumps on Middleside were hit that day. After one of the bombings, someone was playing a small portable AM radio and a reporter from San Francisco announced to his listeners over the air, "We can take anything that the Japs can throw at us." That reporter was the subject of a lot of conversation after that. Everyone wished that he could have been brought to Corregidor so he would understand what was really going on.

"Every time that asshole opens his mouth, the Japs throw everything they have at us," one guy said.

"We should put the SOB in the front seat, just like us, so he can enjoy it all too," another said.

Several soldiers had dug a small cave out of the side of a hill and they were using it for shelter. During one of the shellings, the cave collapsed, killing all eight men inside.

One day, John was looking out towards Bataan and saw a Japanese observation balloon floating in the air. It looked kind of like a balloon with a basket. It was not motorized, but held in position by a cable attached to a winch. At first, he was ready to hide, but then he thought, Oh! what the hell! They already know where I am. So he defiantly stood up, pushed out his right arm and gave them the "Italian salute." Then he thumbed his nose at them.

How the American and Filipino troops could survive the incessant shelling and bombing of Corregidor, no one would ever know. When John had first arrived at Corregidor, there was a lot of green foliage, and even a monkey or two. But after the constant barrages and bombings, everything was cut down. The small island was almost nude of any kind of vegetation. There was just dust and the shambles of wrecked buildings and living quarters. Corregidor was living up to its nickname "the Rock."

The remaining defenders were drawn, beaten and haggard-looking human beings with hopeless looks on their faces. There were days when the soldiers had no food or water, because the soldiers who supplied the food just couldn't get to them with the constant shelling. Sometimes, they would bring the food out of the tunnel at 10 o'clock a night or 4 o'clock in the morning to avoid the heavier bombardments.

By May 1st, the concentration of Japanese artillery fire was in the vicinity of the tail of Corregidor, near where the remnants of John's squad were located at Monkey Point. On May 2nd, during one particularly heavy shelling, the Japanese made a direct hit on two of the artillery batteries on Corregidor, Battery Geary, manned by Americans, and Battery James, manned by Filipino Scouts, blowing them up and killing everyone in them.

On May 3rd, after another particularly heavy artillery barrage, Japanese forces finally landed on the "Tail of the Tadpole." They suffered heavy losses at the hands of the American and Filipino defenders, but they kept coming ashore and were slowly making their way south. On May 4th and 5th, the Japanese increased the level of bombardment, if that were possible, on the rest of the island. During one of these bombings, Company A lost several good men, including Captain Edmund Zbikowski and Privates Chester Bailey, Daniel Daugherty and Sam Drake.

It was very dark on the night of May 5th when another large Japanese assault force came ashore. John was in his foxhole above the small airstrip. He wasn't far from one of the revetments that his squad had built to protect the P-40's. (A revetment is a horseshoe-shaped, protective double wall, about 10 feet high made of corrugated steel and filled with sand. It is designed to protect planes from ground fire, as well as strafing from the air).

There were two 75mm artillery pieces at a place called Hook Point. The location of these two guns was never revealed to the Japanese until the night of the invasion. The Japanese were using a big searchlight from one of the ships to illuminate the two artillery pieces as they fired at the Japanese barges. Americans at Fort Hughes, which was only about 400 feet from John's position, opened up with 12-inch mortars.

The American artillery seemed to be scoring some good hits, and the defense line on the beaches opened up with machine guns. The Japanese invaders were taking heavy losses. The sounds of explosions, machine gun fire, mortars and men calling out in the night were terrifying. Bullets were flying all over the place. A few of them whizzed over John's head, but he didn't know where they were coming from. He decided to dig his foxhole a little deeper using his World War I helmet when Sergeant Kruchowsky yelled to him, "John! Stop making that noise! The Japs are gonna know where the hell you are!" John stopped digging. He stayed as low as he could and fired at the invaders, who were just 100 feet away from his position. The fighting continued throughout the night, but as dawn came, it started to become strangely quiet. Other than some sporadic rifle or machine gun fire, there were no sounds at all. At about 10:30 AM, those that were left from Company A were hunkered down in their foxholes waiting for the next barrage of artillery and bombs. It was eerily quiet. Then, John heard the muffled sounds of people talking. The voices were getting louder and were coming towards his foxhole. He saw an American soldier walking towards his position and waving a white flag.

"What's going on?" John asked him.

"We've surrendered," the soldier said.

"We've what?" John asked in disbelief.

"You heard it right. We've surrendered. The word is that General Wainwright just signed our surrender with one of the Japanese generals."

John couldn't believe it. On the one hand, he felt relieved that he wasn't going to get killed in the bombing, but on the other hand, he was afraid of what lay ahead for him and his fellow soldiers.

"What the hell are we supposed to do now?" John called out, not directing his comments to anyone in particular. Just then, a buck sergeant, who John didn't know, walked over to the small group of ragged-looking soldiers and said, "OK, you all got the word that we've surrendered. It's over for us. Put down your weapons and head down to the Navy's tunnel at the Point. Keep in groups. Don't travel there alone. I don't know what's gonna happen, but stay alert."

The small group left their weapons on the ground and headed down the road towards the tunnel, which was only about 500 feet away from their positions. As they got out onto the road, they could see some wounded Japanese soldiers being treated in hastily-set-up first aid stations down at Cavalry Point near the beach. Jeeps and trucks loaded with Japanese troops drove by, but they seemed to pay very little attention to the Americans and Filipinos.

When they arrived at the Navy tunnel, John and the others went inside to look for any supplies they could find. John managed to find some socks, towels and soap, which he placed in a pillowcase. He took off his wristwatch and put it in his pocket, and he took a ring off of his finger that his sister had given him for his twenty-first birthday. Using a safety pin, he fastened the ring inside his underpants.

A group of about 50 men, from all different outfits and branches of the service, were told to head out for the Malinta Tunnel. They were again reminded to stay in a group. John, like most of the other men in the group, had all of his personal possessions on him. They spotted a group of Japanese soldiers coming on foot from the opposite direction. One of them spotted the pillowcase that John was carrying. Smiling broadly, he walked over and grabbed it from him. Oh well! To the victors belong the spoils! John thought. Other Japanese soldiers were doing the same thing to the other Americans. They even patted down some of the Americans, but they didn't search John. John swore to himself, These bastards are never gonna get my ring! On the short trip to the main tunnel the men were repeatedly searched by roving bands of Japanese soldiers who took anything of value, but they didn't get John's watch or the ring. At least, they didn't get them yet.

Chapter 6

NEW LIFE AS A POW
May 1942

Unwashed, unshaven and weak from a lack of food
and water, small groups of American and Filipino
soldiers, sailors and marines — the remnants of General
Wainwright's army on Corregidor — made their way to
the Malinta Tunnel. As they approached the tunnel,
Japanese soldiers were waiting with fixed bayonets on
their rifles. They were yelling at the American and
Filipino prisoners in Japanese. By threatening to use
their bayonets, they managed to herd these new POW's
into a small area on the east side of the opening of the
tunnel.

Nothing much happened for the rest of that first
day. The men just sat on the ground in the blistering hot
sun watching new stragglers walk into the compound and
awaiting additional orders from their captors. They
mostly just talked about what was happening and what
they thought was going to happen to them in the future.
For many, it was hard to believe that they had actually
surrendered to the Japanese.

The POW's received no food or water that first day, and slept that night in a small area surrounded by Japanese soldiers. During the night, a group of Japanese soldiers walked through the prisoners. As they were passing by, one of the soldiers looked at one of the prisoners who was lying on the ground with his head near the road. He yelled out something in Japanese and then kicked the American POW in the head with his boot. The American never uttered a cry of pain. He just lay there holding his head. Another Japanese soldier then went over to the one who had kicked the POW, and yelled at him. It looked to John like he was bawling him out for kicking the American soldier in the head.

The next morning, the POW's near the Malinta Tunnel were moved down to an area called the 92nd Garage, an outdoor area previously used by the U.S. Navy for storing PBY seaplanes. When John's group arrived at their new location, there was another large group of POW's already there.

The 92nd Garage was a level, concrete-floored area, almost a semi circle in shape, about 500 feet wide at its widest point, and 1500 feet long. It was located between the beach and the cliffs inshore on the southern portion of Corregidor facing out to Cavite. It rapidly filled to overflowing with prisoners of war, both American and Filipino. The only building left standing (if you could call it that) in the area, was the ruins of a garage that had been rendered uninhabitable as a result of the bombing. The Japanese herded the men into groups of 1,000 or so, with an American colonel placed in charge of each group. John just went where he was told.

It was now May 8, 1942, two days after the surrender of Corregidor, and there were approximately

8,000 American and 5,000 Filipino troops being held in or around the 92nd Garage area. By this time, the Japanese guards had managed to rob just about all the prisoners of most of their possessions. Many POW's, however, like John, had hidden some of their more valuable possessions in their undergarments, and these had not been found. Japanese soldiers were walking around proudly displaying and showing each other their new Elgin, Benrus and Waltham wristwatches, and other items taken from the prisoners.

The Japanese issued orders that every prisoner wearing a hat was to salute every Japanese soldier that passed by, and if the POW didn't have a hat on his head, he was to bow at the waist. If a POW didn't salute or bow at the waist when a Japanese soldier passed by, the Japanese would beat him. No food or water was given to the prisoners for the first three days. It was pretty clear that the Japanese were not prepared for so many prisoners. Finally, the Japanese allowed the Americans to install a small pipeline that brought fresh water into the area. The pipe was very small in diameter, only about 1/4 inch, and the men had to stand in line for hours just to fill their canteens. On the fourth day, the Japanese issued a small portion of rice to each man, and after that, an occasional can of food to share amongst several men.

There were no regular toilet facilities in the compound. There were only open latrines, dug by hand in the middle of an area. These areas were swarming with flies and other disease-bearing insects, and the whole compound was really beginning to stink. Nearly all of the prisoners were suffering from dysentery, heat prostration, malaria, malnutrition or other diseases, so the Americans set up a small first aid station which probably kept many of the POW's alive. John had developed some nasty sores so he went to the first aid station where he was treated with Jensen Violet. He looked like a purple eggplant.

Finally, the Japanese allowed the POW's to take a dip in the ocean at the water's edge. No one had the strength to swim away, and most just stood in the water up to their necks. This short dip in the bay cleared up John's sores. It was his first bath in what seemed like ages and it felt pretty good.

The Japanese warned the American and Filipino prisoners that anyone leaving the area would be treated as an escapee and shot on the spot. One Navy guy, named Freddie, tried to escape in a bonca and got caught. He was severely beaten by the Japanese and eventually died of his injuries.

Many of the Filipino soldiers being held in the compound were wearing civilian clothes, which they had quickly changed into after they received word of the surrender. One Filipino soldier wearing civilian clothes had either stashed, or knew of, a supply of U.S. Navy foodstuffs that was located somewhere near the area where the POW's were being held. One afternoon, he took a chance and went to get it. About an hour or so later, he returned to the compound with a white pillowcase full of canned foods. How or where he found it, only he knew. As he passed by the area where John was sitting, a Navy guy jumped up and asked him, "Hey, gook! What you got in the pillowcase?"

"None of your business," the man answered in broken English.

"Come on. Let's see what you got there," the Navy man said as he grabbed at the pillowcase. There was a pushing and showing match, and heated words were being exchanged.

"I said, give me the fucking case!" the Navy man told the Filipino, as he kept him from getting away by holding onto his shirt.

"No, I'm not giving you anything. It's only for me and my friends."

At this point, John stood up and told the Navy guy, "Why don't you leave him alone."

The navy man turned to his buddies and said, "Hey, guys, look! We got a gook-lover over here."

"I'm not a gook-lover or anything else, you asshole! Just leave him alone. He's not the enemy. He's one of us."

Three of the Navy man's shipmates rose up as if to take John on. Just then, an Army officer, Colonel Moore, stood up from his cliffside position and told them, "You guys are still under the control of the United States military. If any of you cause any trouble, I'll see to it that you're all court-martialed." With that, the Navy men just sat down and let the Filipino go on his way.

The next night, the Filipino managed to sneak out again and returned with another pillowcase full of canned foods. He stopped in front of John and said, "Sir, my companions told me to give this to you and to thank you for what you did last night." Then, with the four Navy men watching, he handed John two cans of Del Monte sardines.

"That's not necessary," John told him.

"Sir, this is our way of thanking you. Please take them."

After accepting the two cans of sardines, John threw one can at the four Navy men and told them,

"Remember, we're all still human beings and we are supposed to be in this together."

Each can contained four large sardines, without heads, packed in tomato sauce. When he received his rice rations for the day, John walked over to Colonel Moore and shared his sardines with him. Colonel Moore was one of those individuals who stand out from the crowd. He had thin reddish hair, sharp blue eyes and a deep, commanding voice.

"It was a nice thing you did sticking up for the Filipino, particularly under the circumstances," the Colonel said.

"Thanks Colonel," John replied, managing a faint smile. There wasn't much to smile about on Corregidor, but John felt pretty good about what he had done.

"Where are you from, soldier?" The Colonel asked.

"Brooklyn."

"Oh, you're a New York City guy."

"What about you? Where do you come from?" John asked.

"Cincinnati," Colonel Moore replied.

The two passed the night with small talk. Enlisted men didn't often have the opportunity to sit and talk with officers, but now it was different. The officers and enlisted personnel were all mixed in together. Colonel Moore told John that he had been at Fort Hughes where the 12-inch mortars did quite a bit of damage to the Japanese. He also told John that the Japanese had over 240 artillery pieces firing at Corregidor every day during the siege. He estimated that 16,000 rounds fell on the island every 24 hours.

During their two-plus weeks of captivity on Corregidor, most of the POW's passed the time just watching and waiting. Some, however, were assigned to work details. The prisoners cleaned up gun positions, worked on rebuilding the airfield and the roads, gathered ammunition and loaded the remaining canned foodstuffs onto freighters for transport back to Manila.

Some unlucky POW's were assigned to pick up the dead Japanese soldiers and place them on huge piles of wood. As each dead soldier was brought to the woodpile, a Japanese soldier would cut off a finger. The finger would later be burned to ashes, and then the ashes would be sent back to Japan to be given to the soldier's relatives. The rest of the bodies were burned in huge piles. The POW's assigned to this detail could be seen returning every night covered in dirt, creosote and blood. Sanitary conditions were getting worse. With thousands of POW's confined to a small area, it was becoming pretty rough, and some were starting to get very sick.

Sometime during the afternoon of May 24th, 1942, a Japanese officer speaking in very broken English told the American POW's, "You will be leaving here today. You will be marched down to the dock, and you will be put onto a ship that will take you to your new home." He added, "If any man tries to escape, he will be killed. If any man is caught stealing anything, he will also be killed."

With that, the Japanese guards moved in and began marching the men towards the dock on the south side of the island. As they approached, John could see three Japanese freighters tied up there. While walking on the dock and heading towards one of the ships, John saw a pallet loaded with canned food. Being very careful that no Japanese guards were looking, he reached over, stole an unmarked can of food from the pallet and quickly stuffed it in his shirt. He continued up the ramp to the deck and then walked down the stairs to the hold of the ship.

After settling into his new temporary home, with the aid of a small can opener he opened the can and found that it contained green string beans. He shared the contents with a fellow member of the 803rd Engineers and a Navy man. They each took one string bean at a time. After finishing the beans, they shared the liquid in the can.

More than 1,000 POW's were herded into the hold of this ship. It was almost impossible to stand or to move about, but all in all the conditions were not that bad. They spent the night aboard the freighter. On the morning of May 25th, the transport ships pulled up anchor, and about six hours later, they arrived at a place called Langley Point, which is near Cavite. After the transport anchored offshore, the men were made to scramble down a rope ladder onto Japanese motorized landing barges that carried about 50 men each. The barges took them to a point that was about 100 yards from shore. Then, they were told to jump in the water, which was about four feet deep, and walk to the beach.

The prisoners, all Americans at this point, were then assembled in columns of four. John was the only guy from the 803rd Engineers that was in his group. The men were herded and kept in line by mounted Japanese cavalrymen. Then, they began their march up Dewey Boulevard towards Manila and Bilbid Prison, which was about five miles away. It was very hot and some of the POW's were in such bad shape that they couldn't even make it the first mile.

Of course, the Japanese were taking a lot of pride in showing off the American prisoners. It was obvious to John that the Japanese were marching the prisoners through the streets in an attempt to show the Filipino people that the Japanese forces were superior to the Americans. John noticed that the Filipinos who were watching the prisoners march by had very sorrowful looks on their faces.

John saw an elderly Filipino woman with tears running down her cheeks. Holding her fingers near her mouth, she made a "V" sign for victory as the prisoners passed by, and John managed to return a faint smile. A young Filipino boy was running from one side of the road to the other handing out water to anyone who was lucky enough to pass by him. Many of the Filipino people standing in the streets tried to give food, candy or cigarettes to the prisoners. Those that were caught doing so were struck by the Japanese with fists or with the butts of rifles.

At one point during the march, the group was ordered to stop. As they did, one of the Japanese cavalry soldiers dismounted from his horse and ordered a Filipino boy to bring him some water. When the water was brought over, the guard took his helmet off, poured the water into it and then gave it to his horse to drink. What a feeling of hopelessness came over John! He thought, Their goddamned horses come before us. These Jap bastards don't give a damm about us.

As the POW's were passing through a small barrio, John happened to look up and saw a white woman looking down from an open window. John couldn't help staring. For some reason, he just couldn't take his eyes off her. Maybe it was because she was the first white woman he had seen in months. In any case, he kept looking at her until their eyes finally met. John was puzzled to see a white woman who was not interned by the Japanese, and he yelled out in her direction, "Oh, for a ham sandwich!" Then he thought, What a dope! Why the hell did I yell that out? It sounded really stupid, even to him.

"Do you see that white woman up there?" he asked the guy next to him, who was a regular Army man from the 31st Infantry.

"Yeah, she's probably a white Russian. There's quite a few of them around here in the Philippines. They're not at war with the Japs so I guess they're still free."

It was now late afternoon. The group passed a cross street named Azcarranga Avenue and turned into a stone-covered courtyard. As they got closer, the massive iron gates of Bilbid Prison swung open, allowing the tired marchers to enter an inner courtyard space. The men could see a stone guardhouse on the left, and a very large, very old, three-story building with a tower that straddled the only narrow entrance to the main, high-walled prison. Bilbid Prison was a penitentiary built by the Spanish almost two centuries earlier, and was most recently used to house convicted Filipino criminals before the war.

John's group was marched through the first part of the prison through a narrow entranceway and into the section which was now housing POW's. This would be their home for a few days or a week. During these days, just about everything John possessed, with the exception of that one ring given to him by his sister, would be stolen by other American POW's. He couldn't understand how

Americans could do this to other Americans. He learned a very valuable lesson, however, and would always become suspicious in the future when someone came around to his area or was admiring his possessions.

After almost a week at Bilbid, a Japanese officer notified the men through an interpreter that a group of about five hundred POW's would be leaving the next day. The next morning, John and the others in this group were marched to the railroad station in Manila. When they arrived, they could see that the railroad cars and tracks were quite a bit smaller than those in America. The freight cars were very small, maybe twenty feet long, and made of wood. Some of the cars had solid walls and some had small openings in them. The Japanese packed the POW's in so tightly that they all had to stand. The doors were slammed shut, but the train stayed in the station for quite a while.

Finally, the train began to move. Then, they made a short stop at a place called San Fernando. The Japanese guards opened the doors, but the men were not allowed to leave the cars. Local Filipinos threw some foodstuffs towards the prisoners, and a few lucky ones caught them. John was not one of them.

The Japanese soldiers locked the doors again, and they began moving. It was a pretty rough ride and several of the men passed out. It was hot and stuffy in the closed railroad cars. Some of the men had to urinate where they stood. John was wearing his long, Army khaki pants, khaki shirt and his work boots. He had no canteen, or any other means to carry water, because his canteen had been stolen in Bilbid Prison.

The train stopped at a place called Cabanatuan, in Tarlac Province. The POW's were then marched in two groups of two hundred and fifty or so, in columns of four, towards a former Filipino Army training camp called Camp #3. On this march, John saw four Americans die. On one occasion, John saw a Navy man lying prostrate on the ground, apparently passed out from the march. A Japanese soldier walked up and nudged the POW with his bayonet. When he didn't get any reaction, he then repeatedly stabbed the man until he was sure he was dead. Another American POW had to urinate. Because he was afraid to stop, he decided to do it while he was walking. As he was urinating, a Japanese soldier ran up behind him and stuck him in the shoulder with his bayonet. The men were all shocked and the line of march actually stopped. The guard made a gesture indicating that if the man had to piss, he should have stepped out of line to do it.

As the group continued their march, John and his fellow POW's could see candy bars, cans of food and other small items along the road, apparently left there by local Filipinos. At one point, the men spotted a pair of tan pants along the roadside. After seeing one guy get bayoneted for urinating, most of the men were reluctant to step out of line for any reason.

"Man, look at those pants!" John said to the guy next to him.

"They look pretty new," the guy answered.

"I'm gonna try and get them."

"Don't be a fool. If they see you, they'll probably kill you."

"I don't give a shit. I'm gonna get them." With that, John ran out of the line, grabbed the pants and jumped back without the Japanese noticing. In the pants, which turned out to be brand new, John found a ten peso note, which he guessed must have been left there on purpose by a Filipino.

During the long march, John became very thirsty. He had no canteen, and it was very hot. A first sergeant, who had two canteens on his web belt, one on each side, was marching nearby and saw John's plight.

"Hey, kid. Where's your canteen?" the first sergeant asked.

"It was stolen in Bilbid," John told him.

"Don't you have any water at all?"

"No."

"Here. Take a swig out of mine," the first sergeant said as he gave him a drink from his canteen.

"Thanks," John said. "I really appreciate it."

As the group continued to march, the weaker ones couldn't keep up and started to fall behind. John kept moving up towards the front of the group. Eventually, the first group arrived and entered the small compound, which was not far away from where John had helped build an airstrip before the war started.

Camp #3 was located on a couple of hundred acres of fairly flat land near the O'Donnell River. It was on the eastern side of the central plain of Luzon, formerly rice paddies at the foot of the Sierra Madre Mountains. Camp #3 had been built a few months before the war as the headquarters and training area of a Philippine Army division. There were about four or five large wood and bamboo barracks thatched with cogan grass, and with walls of sawali or nipa in woven sections. Many of the framed panels were hinged and could be propped open to catch a breeze and allow a view outside. The camp, which was surrounded with barbed wire, had a main gate fronting on the road that led from the nearby town of Cabanatuan.

Within the large main compound were smaller compounds — three for the prisoners, one for the Japanese guards, and one for the hospital. John was one of the first POW's to get into one of the new compound areas. He used his cupped hands to drink water from a spigot. For some reason, the guards were keeping the others outside of the compound, and the line of marchers was backing up. Many of the POW's were lined up sticking their canteens and water bottles through the fence, calling to John to fill their containers. John saw the first sergeant who had given him a drink of water during the march. He yelled to him, "Hey, Sarge. Come on up to the front and I'll fill up your canteen first."

"Hey, what are you doing?" one POW said.

"We were here before him," another said.

"Why is he getting filled up first?" others yelled.

"Where were you guys when I was dying of thirst on the march?" John replied. "He was the only one who would give me a drink from his canteen and he comes first. If you don't let him in front, no one gets anything!"

With that, the first sergeant was allowed to come to the front and give John his canteen. John filled the canteen and they smiled at each other. After john filled a couple of the other canteens, the Japanese guards finally let the rest of the POW's into the compound.

The prisoners lived in the nipa shacks packed in like sardines on three levels. The barracks building was built like the shell of a house and it was not very strong. When rain and wind came, the whole building swayed. Because John was on the third level, it seemed to him to sway even more that it actually did. The men were fed one mess kit-full of rice per day. The pants he had found along the road were too small for John, so he gave them to the first sergeant who had given him the drink of water (but he kept the ten pesos). John was beginning to learn how to survive as a POW.

Those that didn't have mess kits when they arrived in Camp #3 received them from the Japanese. A POW from the 803rd Engineers, Felix Kozakevitch, etched a crucifix and the prayers for before and after meals on the lid, and a portrait of Jesus with the sacred heart on the inside, of John's new mess kit. Before being drafted, Felix Kozakevitch had lived on Jewel Street in Greenpoint, not far from John's apartment house. He told John he wanted to study to be an architect after the war. When John went to receive his rations one day, the guy who was dishing out the food saw the etchings on his canteen cover and said. "That's some sweetheart you got there!"

John's answer to this guy was, "The best." He never told the guy it was a picture of Jesus.

Punishment was very harsh at the camp. When the guards caught a POW stealing food one day, they placed his hand on one brick and his forearm on another. Then they struck his wrist with a 2x4, breaking it.

On another occasion, four Americans were caught trying to escape. First, they were forced to dig their own graves. Then they were tied to posts in front of the graves, where they stayed until sunset. At that point, the other POW's were ordered to stay inside the barracks, close all openings and not look out. John decided to take a chance and look out anyway, and he was shocked by what he saw.

He could see the Americans tied to the posts in front of their graves, and he could hear them singing "God Bless America" as the Japanese firing squad was aiming at them. The Japanese officer in charge yelled out an order, shots rang out and the four POW's went limp. They were cut from the posts and fell into the graves. To John's surprise, one of the four rose up and pointed to his forehead, asking the Japanese officer to finish him off. The officer fired his gun and the American fell backwards. Then, the officer went to each grave and fired one more round into each of the Americans.

While going to the latrine one day, John ran into John Delamater from upstate New York, who was in Company A with him. Delamater, a nice quiet guy, was older than most of the others in the camp, having been drafted when he was thirty-five. Delamater had become very ill and weak with dysentery and had developed a bad case of the runs. He did not have the strength to walk back and forth from his nipa shack, and because he was so weak, he decided to stay close to the slit trench. John felt very sorry for him. The 'blow flies' — big greenish flies — were all over his lips, nostrils, eyelids and the wet part of his pants.

"You got to get out of here; you're covered with flies." John told Delamater.

"I know," Delamater replied. He was so weak he could hardly talk.

"Let me take you back."

"No. Thanks anyway, but I just want to stay here."

"If you stay here, you're not going to make it," John told him.

"Johnny, what can I do? Every time I get back to the shack I gotta go again. So then I have to come back here. I don't have the strength to go back and forth all day and night, and I just don't care anymore," Delamater said in a very weak voice.

John felt sorry for his friend but he was in no position to help him. He was barely alive himself, and it was all he could manage to keep himself going. He never saw John Delamater again, but later learned that he had become weaker, was taken to the camp hospital and died.

John, like many of the other prisoners, learned to treat himself for various ailments. A tropical ulcer about the size of a dime was growing on the calf of his left leg. A POW from Tennessee told him that his mother used to use brown soap mixed with tree sap as a homemade ointment. John found some soap, mixed it with some tree sap into a paste, and put it on. The ulcer healed in a week.

For some reason, John decided to wear the ring his sister had given him while he was on his first bathing detail. After he came out of the river, he noticed a real cruddy-looking Japanese guard eyeing him. It didn't occur to him right away that the guard was looking at the ring on his finger. A few minutes later, the guard motioned to John to go with him. He took John out of sight of the others and pointed at his hand. He wanted the ring, but John said no. The guard pointed his bayonet at John. He realized that he was at the guard's mercy. All this guy has to do is shoot me, take the ring and say that I tried to escape, John thought. There was nothing else he could do, so he gave the SOB the ring.

One night, there was a commotion outside of the barracks. Guys were talking and their voices were getting louder and louder. Finally, John decided to go out to see what was going on. Everyone was looking skyward. Then he saw it. It was a "Blue Moon." He had never seen anything like this before. The moon had a bluish-green color. One of the guys told him it was because of the evaporation of seawater. But it didn't matter what caused it, John only knew it was beautiful.

One Sunday, John could hear a song being sung by a group of Americans sitting on the ground inside of the compound. They were singing, "Holy, Holy, Holy, Lord God Almighty." He went over, sat down and listened to the Protestant chaplain. Even though John was a Roman Catholic, he felt that he just had to be there. He was given a booklet to read, which he tried to read every day.

While he was reading the prayers one day, a POW from Pennsylvania who looked a little like the actor Lee VanCleef turned to John and said, "Here, Johnny, keep these. You'll have more use for them than I will." Then he gave John a pair of the most beautiful, dark ruby-red rosary beads he ever saw. He told John that his mother had sent them to him.

John couldn't understand why the guy gave them to him. The rosary beads would later be stolen from John by a fellow POW.

In August of 1942, the Japanese began moving the prisoners from Camp #3 to Camp #1 at Cabanatuan. After arriving at Camp #1, John met many of the men who had been captured on Bataan and had participated in the "Death March." During this time, John also met some other members of the 803rd Engineers. One guy from Company B told him that American POW's on Bataan were made to stand in front of the Japanese artillery while they were building the gun emplacements and while they were shelling Corregidor. Many times, when the American forces on Corregidor shelled the Japanese artillery positions on Bataan, they killed Americans. When the Americans on Corregidor found out what was happening, they stopped the shelling.

The prisoners taken on Bataan told John that after they were captured, they were all searched. If anyone was found with Japanese money in his possession, he was beheaded. The Japanese did this because they assumed that if a POW had anything Japanese in his possession, he must have taken it from a dead Japanese soldier. The POW's on Bataan were marched with no food and little water for several days. They were made to sit in the boiling sun, continually beaten by the Japanese troops and not permitted to lie down at night. Prisoners too weak to continue, many of them sick and delirious, were killed if they fell out of line. In one case, a POW fell down on the road and a Japanese tank drove over him and crushed him into the road. Some went crazy on the march, and many more died on the way and in the camp.

John was told that just before he arrived at Camp #1 three American officers had tried to escape: Lt. Col. Biggs, Lt. Col. Reitung and Lt. Gilert, USN. The Japanese stripped them, tied them to a post in front of the camp gate, and forced passing Filipinos to beat them across the face with a 2 x 4 board. The officers were kept in the blazing sun for 2 days without water. Two were shot dead, and Lt. Col. Biggs was beheaded. The Japanese guards put the American officer's head on a pole and marched around the camp with it until ordered by a Japanese officer to stop.

The guards at Camp #1 routinely beat and kicked the prisoners on the slightest excuse or, indeed, without any excuse at all. The members of the prison farm detail suffered especially from brutal treatment at the hands of their guards. Every supervisor carried a short club or golf stick that they did not hesitate to use indiscriminately on the prisoners whenever they felt like it. In many instances, a wholesale campaign of beatings and torture was visited on the farm detail for no cause whatsoever.

The Japanese camp commander issued the so-called "shooting squad" order, according to which all men in the camp were divided into squads of ten men each. If any one of the ten succeeded in escaping, the other nine were to be summarily executed in reprisal. Some prisoners, afraid they would be killed if someone else escaped, would tell the Japanese guards about planned escapes.

In one case, an American POW saw two other Americans trying to escape into the jungle. He sounded the alarm. The Japanese caught the two Americans a short time later. The American commander tried to convince the Japanese that the two POW's were very sick and didn't know what they were doing, but the Japanese commander did not buy the story and the two Americans were shot. It was a kind of "Catch-22" situation for the POW who sounded the alarm. If he didn't yell out and the two POW's successfully escaped, ten other POWs would surely have been killed by the Japanese. It could not have been an easy decision.

The food at Cabanatuan consisted of half a cup of lugao (rice gruel) twice daily, and a dipper-full of oiled "whistle weed," or even mongo beans sometimes. Possibly once monthly, a carabao (water buffalo) would be killed, which would serve to faintly color the rice gruel. One old animal did little to enhance 6,000 soup rations.

Some of the prisoners at this camp had managed to scrounge up enough parts to put together a short-wave radio, and the prisoners heard that on August 7, 1942, U.S. forces had made their first offensive landing against the Japanese at Guadalcanal in the Solomon Islands. Rumors were flying that the Japanese were going to be moving large numbers of prisoners to Japan and China.

It finally happened in September of 1942. The Japanese were looking for volunteers, and initially took about five hundred prisoners out. A couple of guys who "volunteered" to go knew John, and they asked him to go along, telling him that anything had to be better than this. But John declined, saying, "I'm not volunteering for anything."

In early October of 1942, John and about 500 other POW's were taken out of Camp #1 and marched to the train. The same conditions existed on this train ride as the one before it — crowded, filthy, stuffy, with hardly any air. The train reached Manila, and the men were made to march to the dock. The dock was called Pier Seven, which was the Million-Dollar Pier, the same place the Tasker H. Bliss docked when John first arrived in the Philippines.

The men all boarded a large transport and were put down in the hold. There was no food or water that night, and the ship did not move until the following day. Once outside of Manila Bay, the Japanese allowed the POW's to go topside during the day to get some air. While they were on the deck, the Japanese hosed the POW's down with fire hoses. It felt pretty good. John noticed that the Japanese crew had a large pig in a cage that they were feeding with scraps from their mess hall. They also hosed down his cage with the hose. On one occasion during this trip, the Japanese conducted target practice with their cannon.

The ship was moving very slowly and hugging the coastline. One day, John had a conversation with a Japanese crew member while he was on the deck. Although the conversation was in "pigeon English" and broken Japanese, they somehow managed to communicate with each other. The Japanese sailor talked about a great sea battle he had seen. He spoke highly of the American warships. He described the shelling as "pom-pom", the American warship as "goodos" and an allied warship as "domei," meaning "no good." He told John that the guns of the American warship were still firing as the ship was going down. He asked John if he had been on Bataan or Corregidor. When John replied that he had been in both places, the sailor said "goodo." John knew that the Japanese admired people who had been in battle and considered them to be warriors. The prison ships then anchored for one night off the coast of Cebu, where Magellan had been killed.

Chapter 7

DAVAO
October 1942

After a few days, the freighter dropped anchor at a place called Davao (pronounced Da-vow). The port of Davao is located in a large indentation of the southern coast of Mindanao, the southernmost island of the Philippine group. The POW's climbed down the rope ladders from the freighters into small motor launches that took them near the shore. They climbed out of the launches, waded ashore and were lined up.

A Japanese officer walked to the front of the group and spoke through an interpreter: "Put all of your belongings in the truck. They will be given back to you when you arrive at the camp." The men did as they were told, then returned to the formation to await further instructions. Shortly thereafter, the POW's were given the order to move out and they began their march to their new home. Along the way, they passed by some native huts and noticed that many of the local people had Japanese features. The women even wore their hair in buns like Japanese women.

The prisoners arrived in Camp Davao in the early evening. It had taken them almost seven hours to walk the fifteen or so miles to their new home. When the truck containing the personal possessions finally arrived, the men were told to go get their belongings. Unfortunately for John, the "vultures" had been waiting for the truck. When John finally got to the truck, his belongings were nowhere to be found. I can't believe it, John thought. How can Americans steal from other Americans? Also during that very first evening, the Japanese confiscated all of the shoes and boots that belonged to the POW's, in order to prevent them from escaping. The only personal possession John had left at this point was his mess kit with the picture of Jesus on it, which was the only item he had kept with him since landing outside of Davao earlier that day. It took him about a week, but he somehow managed to get some clothing and a blanket. He was very angry at what had happened, and became very suspicious of his fellow POW's.

Camp Davao had formerly been a penal institution for Filipino civilian offenders. It was located in a region of swamps and jungles. There were eight main prisoner barracks in the area. Each structure was about 125 feet long and 50 feet wide. They were made of wood planking, with openings for windows, and corrugated tin roofs with five-foot overhangs. There were a couple of smaller buildings that were used as a church, POW headquarters, a kitchen and a hospital.

Fruit trees of many varieties grew in abundance in the area just outside of the camp. The camp was surrounded by barbed wire, and outside of the barbed wire perimeter lived the Japanese guards and Filipino workers. The water supply for the prison came from artesian wells in the vicinity of the camp. Water from these wells was pumped into three tanks set on towers within the compound, and then carried by force of gravity through pipes to faucets in the camp. Camp Davao was, by far, the cleanest of all the prison camps that John had been in. When the group first arrived in the camp, there were no showers. The men simply filled up a bucket of water and poured it over their heads. Before the POW's came, the previous Filipino civilian prisoners raised chickens and pigs, but now it grew rice, tropical fruits and vegetables.

The total POW population at Davao was just over 2,000. Shortly before John's group arrived at Davao, another group of POW's had arrived from Del Monte Field. Contrary to the physical condition of some of the other POW's, the group from Del Monte Field looked pretty healthy, as if they had been well fed. The lieutenant in charge of John's barracks had come from Del Monte Field, and he was still quite overweight. He was given the nickname "the white elephant" by the guys in the barracks. One of the guys assigned to John's barracks, Private Joe Burke from the Army Air Corps, had a picture of the Americans surrendering in formation at Del Monte Field.

The men quickly learned a few Japanese words like "kiotski," which meant "attention." Every morning they would fall out for "tinko" (roll call and inspection) and count off in Japanese. The men rehearsed their counting off in the barracks, and always stood in the same place in formation so they would know how to say their number in Japanese.

In those first days at Camp Davao, the POW's were told that they would get to eat any food that they could grow. For the first couple of months, while the Japanese were doing well in the war, the POW's received a fair ration of rice and vegetables, and on some occasions, strings of meat. The Japanese would give the American POW cooks the front legs of water buffalo. If the men were lucky, when the rice and broth were doled out, they might get a small string of meat mixed in. Tea was served with each meal. When the regular tea ran out, tea was made with ginger roots. On some occasions, the Japanese gave the men kelp (seaweed), camotes (a type of sweet potato), casaba (tapioca) and squash, which was cooked into a soup consistency.

The work details started very early at Camp Davao. The POW's would get up from their assigned positions on the wooden floor of their barracks before sunrise and go down to the kitchen to get their portion of rice and a canteen cup of tea. Each day, the Japanese officers would tell the American POW commander, Colonel Olson, how many men they needed for each detail, and Colonel Olson would make the assignments. In the beginning, the commissioned officer POW's would get the details where they could get some extra food. The enlisted POW's called this "quan," which in Filipino meant "anything." The Japanese did not care who did what work. All they cared about was that if a job called for fifty men, they get fifty men to do it.

After a couple of work details out in the jungle, John came down with beriberi. He had severe pain in his fingers and toes. It felt like someone was cutting him with a knife. He wound up in the "Bioki," or sick ward.

The Japanese prison camp commander, Colonel Mori, had owned a bicycle store in Manila before the war. He was one of many Japanese nationals that the

Japanese had "planted" in the Philippines before the war. Under his command, conditions at the camp were not too bad.

On Christmas day in 1942, the Japanese gave the POW's a day off. There were no work details, and the men were given extra rations. They were even given some old magazines, like Cosmopolitan. John was still in the Bioki on Christmas day, still suffering from the effects of beriberi. In the afternoon, Colonel Mori came in to visit and asked the POW's to sing some Christmas carols. Although they thought the request was a bit strange, John and five of his fellow prisoners sang "Oh Little Town of Bethlehem" and a few other Christmas songs. After they finished, Colonel Mori gave each of them a long, brown, thin cigar called a "dobie." John didn't smoke, so he traded his for some other thing he could use. Later that evening, Major Hart, an American POW, came into the Bioki and told the men the story of Horatio Hornblower.

Two or three hundred POW's in the camp had contracted beriberi. There were two kinds of beriberi — the wet one and the dry one. The wet one caused the stomach and legs to swell, which caused severe pain, and the dry one caused excruciating pain in the fingers and toes. One day, a good-looking Japanese doctor came over to John and asked him in perfect English, "Hey Joe, how do you feel?"

"Not so great. I have a lot of pain in my joints," John replied.

Just then, one of the American medical officers came over and told the Japanese doctor, "If the prisoners do not get some Vitamin B-1 in their diet, the problem is going to get worse."

The Japanese doctor solved this problem by giving the men polishings from the rice. The polishings, which are rich in vitamin B-1, came from the brown part of the rice that the Japanese guards usually fed to the animals because the Japanese only liked white rice. On orders from the Japanese doctor, John and his fellow beriberi sufferers were given three-quarters of a canteen cup full of rice polishings each day, which they mixed into a paste with water. Within two weeks, John had recovered and was able to return to the work details.

There was an 18-year-old young man from Massachusetts, Elmer Searle, who was in the Bioki with John. Elmer was always joking around. He had been assigned to a gun emplacement at Nichols Field. When Japanese bombers scored a direct hit on the emplacement and blew it up, Elmer was the only one who survived.

In the camp, every time it thundered during a storm, Elmer would become very excitable and nervous, and start to shake. Every time he did this, a couple of the wise guys in the Bioki would laugh. John was getting madder by the minute because he knew why Elmer was acting the way he was. The guys who were laughing had been stationed at Del Monte Field and had never seen combat. John was now almost fully recovered from his bout with beriberi, and he couldn't stand it anymore. He stood up, turned to the guys that were laughing and said, "The next son-of-a-bitch who laughs at this kid, I'll knock on his ass!" Everyone got quiet.

The Japanese guards counted the men when they left the camp in the morning on various work details, and they counted them when they returned. The first few days without their shoes had been pretty rough on the men's feet, and John was no exception. Every little stone he stepped on caused pain. Eventually, his feet became tough and callused.

While on these work details, John and his fellow POW's managed to grab fruit hanging from trees and eat it. The Japanese were keeping the POW's on pretty much of a "no-frills" diet, giving them just enough to stay alive. Stealing and eating fruit from the trees became a way of life for the men of the camp. Of course, if the prisoners were caught eating fruit on the work details or bringing some "quan" back to camp, they would be beaten by the guards

One day during the rainy season, a typhoon struck. There were high winds and it was raining very heavily. All the work details had been cancelled, except the detail assigned to harvest rice at the Mac Tan rice field. The Japanese insisted that the rice had to be harvested. So, three to four hundred American POW's went out to the rice fields that day. Around four o'clock in the afternoon, those who were back at Camp Davao began to hear muffled noises way off in the distance that sounded like singing. Many of the men in the camp came out of their barracks as the sounds got louder. They saw the returning Americans pushing the small gauge train because it couldn't get traction on the wet tracks. Those in the camp just stood there in amazement as the sounds of the singing men came closer to the camp.

As the work detail approached the front gate, their fellow POW's could recognize the tune. John will never forget the sight: Americans marching four across, soaking wet, cold and hungry (they had not been fed all day), singing "God Bless America" as they marched into the compound. It made John feel very proud. Colonel Mori issued an order to give every man who had been on the

Mac Tan rice detail half a coconut. He obviously admired these brave men for their spirit in the face of the beating they had taken from the weather that day.

The prisoners never knew what details they would be working on from one day to the next. The lieutenant in charge of each barracks would call out the names of the men and tell them what details they were going on. If hundreds of men were assigned to a particular work detail on a given day, the men knew it would be a tough day for them. In John's barracks, the lieutenant and the sergeant never went out on work details. As was the practice in most of the barracks, if the men wanted to be assigned to good details, they had to give some "quan" to the sergeants in the barracks.

John was assigned to a wide variety of details. He worked as a farmhand planting squash and cassava. Cassava is a starchy root from which tapioca is made. Lieutenant Gentry, who had majored in agricultural studies at the University of Kentucky, was in charge of the "squash detail." In order to pollinate the squash, the POW's had to take a male plant and lightly brush it against the female plant because there were not enough bees to do the job. John also worked in the rice bodega (warehouse) milling and sacking rice, which was considered to be a pretty good detail. He also worked on the firewood detail and as a "Squee-gee," a Japanese K.P. While assigned to the Mac Tan rice field, John learned to plow, harrow and harvest the rice paddy. He also learned how to handle a water buffalo. Here he was, a kid from Brooklyn holding onto a water buffalo and plowing the rice fields.

John's first day working in the Mac Tan rice fields started off with a fight. The American group leader told

John what to do and where to get his plow. John went over to where he saw two plows lying together. When he started to pick one out, a POW named Nelson, who was standing next to the plows, told him, "Leave the plow alone. I'm saving it for my friend."

"Where's your friend?" John asked.

"He's on his way," Nelson said. As John started to take the plow anyway, Nelson pushed him away.

"I told you I'm saving this plow for my friend."

"I don't give a shit who you're saving it for. I was told to come over here and get a plow, and that's what I'm doing," John replied. The two men were standing nose to nose in the rice paddy, which was soft with oozing mud.

"I'll beat the shit out of you if you touch that plow," Nelson said. Then the two swung at each other almost simultaneously. John hit Nelson in the mouth with two quick jabs, knocking him down. Blood was coming from his mouth and nose.

"You better stay down and cool off. If you get up, I'll kill you," John said. Nelson knew enough to stay down.

They looked around and saw that the Japanese guards on the dikes were watching but they weren't doing anything about it. Realizing that their fight was serving as entertainment for the guards, the two men cooled off and shook hands.

One fellow who had seen the fight started to rave about how John had lowered the boom on the other guy, and John told him, "Keep quiet about what happened. I don't want to get a reputation as some kind of a rooster. If you tell anybody what happened, I'll lower the boom on you." John and Nelson eventually became friendly and there were no more hard feelings.

One day, four enlisted men were assigned to work with several American officers on the wood-chopping detail because there weren't enough officers available who weren't sick. Officers usually had the better details, so the enlisted men were looking forward to it. The captain in charge of the detail stood in front of the enlisted men prior to going out into the field and said,

"Listen to me. I want to make myself perfectly clear. No one is to bring back any quan to the compound for lunch. You'll wait until you come back in the afternoon." To emphasize the point he yelled, "Is that clear enough? Do the four of you understand me?"

The men nodded in agreement and the group left for the fields, which weren't from the camp. About noon, the detail returned to the compound for lunch. While sitting down eating his bowl of rice, one of the enlisted man who was on the detail with John turned to John and said, "Hey, look over there. The friggin' officers brought back some fruit and are eating it."

"Well, I'm gonna find out if its true." John got up and went over to the front of the officers' quarters to confront the captain in charge of the detail.

"Hey, Captain, why are you and the other officers allowed to bring quan back to the compound, but we're not?" John asked, trying to hold back his anger. "Didn't you tell us that no one was to bring back any quan until the afternoon?" John asked. When the officer ignored the question and didn't answer right away, John added, "You're a no-good son-of-a-bitch! You lied to us."

"Do you realize who you're talking to?" the officer finally said.

"Yeah, I know who I'm talking to — a two-faced, lying sack of shit. That's who I'm talking to."

"You better watch your language, Private."

"Yeah! Or what?" John challenged.

The officer stood up and made a motion like he was going to hit John.

"If you take a swing at me, I'll kill you, you son-of-a-bitch!" John yelled out, as he looked the officer straight in the eye. Then John spotted the officer's military ring with the dark stone and told him, "I thought officers were supposed to be gentlemen."

That got to the officer and he said, "Come with me. You're going to see Colonel Olson."

The captain took John over to the barracks where the American POW commander, Colonel Olson had his command post. The captain went in first and told John to stay outside. Other guys were walking by wondering why John was standing outside the commander's building. One of them yelled out jokingly as he passed by, "Hey John. How come you're going to the principal's office? What did you do?"

As John waited impatiently outside, he could hear the officer telling the colonel that John had threatened him and was disrespectful towards him. Just wait till I get in there and the colonel hears what this officer did to us, John thought.

Then the Colonel yelled out, "Come on in here, Private Mackowski!" When John walked in, Colonel Olson asked him, "Did you talk to this officer that way?"

"What way is that, Sir?" John asked.

"Did you call the captain a son-of-a-bitch?"

"Yes I did, Colonel, because he is a no-good, lying son-of-a-bitch. As far as I'm concerned, he's not an officer, or a gentleman either. He told all of us enlisted men that nobody could take any quan back to the camp for lunch, and then all of the officers took some back with them."

"You can't talk to an officer like that," Colonel Olson said.

"But Colonel, he screwed all of us enlisted men. It's not fair."

"It doesn't matter. You can't talk to an officer like that."

Colonel Olson did not want to listen to John's explanation any more and he ordered John's barracks leader, the white elephant, "Give Private Mackowski latrine guard duty for two weeks because of his disrespectful actions toward an officer." This special guard duty was to be performed after John's regular working detail, and it ran from around 8:00PM to midnight.

In the beginning, the only sources of information were rumors and the Japanese camp newspaper, Co-Asia Prosperity, which was always filled with propaganda about how well Japan was doing in the war. After a while, the Japanese stopped giving the newspaper to the POW's after they caught some using it to wipe their backsides after a bowel movement. In regard to the rumors, the men in the camp had a favorite expression, "What seat did you get it off?" This referred to the seats in the latrine that had been named after KGEI, a well-known radio station in San Francisco.

As things started to get rough for the Japanese, they began to cut the rice rations for the POW's. The POW's were growing the food, and the Japanese were sending much of it to their troops in Davao. The POW's knew things were not going well for the Japanese. The Americans had managed to make a homemade radio out of spare parts. The Japanese always sent a couple of POW's down to their motor pool in Davao to help keep their vehicles running. While there, the Americans would steal bits and pieces of radio parts, and they eventually managed to build a short-wave radio. The POW's learned about the battles of Midway, the Solomon Islands and the Coral Sea, and that the Italians had surrendered.

There was a Japanese interpreter called Mr. Wada who had the nickname of "Running Water" because he always appeared to be trotting behind the Japanese officer in charge. When a POW asked Mr. Wada if it was true that the Italians had surrendered, Mr. Wada told the officer in charge that the POW's must have a radio. The Japanese searched the camp, but couldn't find it. Only a handful of POW's knew where the radio (or radios) were stashed because of the fear that some POW might give up the location in return for some favor from the Japanese. Therefore, only a few had first-hand knowledge of what was going on in the world. The rest were left with no alternative but to get their information through the rumor mill.

Some of the guards at Davao were given nicknames by the POW's. There was "Five O'clock Shadow," a guard who always looked like he needed a shave. Another was called "Betty Boop" because he had a face that resembled the actress Helen Kane. "The Bull" was a well-built guard who looked like a weight lifter. "Mickey Mouse" looked very much like the cartoon character. "Wax Dummy" was a name given to a Japanese officer who had very shiny skin and walked ramrod straight. Rumor had it that he came from a very wealthy family, but had disgraced himself in China by running away from the fighting. Then there was "Bulb Nose" who had a very big nose. "Little Caesar" was Lieutenant Hashimoto, one of the ranking officers in the camp. He made a lot of noise and strutted around all the time.

To get extra food or any other items of value, most of the POW's were willing to take chances to steal them. Even a bent nail lying on the ground could be worth something to someone. Maybe it could be exchanged for something else of value. If the POW's got caught, they were usually beaten by the guards. When a prisoner received a beating, the POW's called it a "strafe job." If a POW had never received a beating, he was called "cherry."

John lost his cherry when he was beaten for stealing a can of Del Monte sardines from the bodega. John was wearing a denim jacket at the time. (He wore the jacket to conceal quan, not because it was cold). This particular day, he tried to conceal the can of sardines by putting it under his left armpit. As the POW's were leaving the bodega, someone in the front of the group was caught concealing two stolen bottles of San Miguel beer from the Japanese lieutenant's private stock, so the Japanese held a showdown of all the POW's.

One guard noticed the outline of the sardine can under John's armpit and pointed to it. When John didn't respond fast enough, the guard punched him in the head. John saw a lot of colors when he was hit. He thought it was the hardest punch he had received in quite a while. The guard then ordered John to put the can back, which he did. As he was coming out the door, the guard was searching the other POW's, so John reached over and grabbed two handfuls of brown sugar from an open gunnysack and stuffed it into his right pants pocket.

He went outside and stood in formation with the rest of the detail. The guard came out, looked John over and said something in Japanese. Then they were all marched back to the compound. When they returned to the compound, a POW started to needle John, saying, "Hey guys, the Polack just lost his cherry."

John took it in stride. He put his hand in his pocket, pulled out a fist full of brown sugar, turned to the guy who had made the comment and said, "Up your ass."

"John, how the hell can you steal something right after getting strafed for stealing?" one of them asked.

"I'm not going to let that Jap bastard hit me for nothing," John replied. Every POW had their moments, and this was one of John's best.

Stealing from the Japanese and "wheeling and dealing" for items was becoming a way of life for most Americans in the prison camps, and John was becoming pretty good at it. In time, John became known as one of the many wheeler dealers who would steal from the Japanese and trade it with other POW's. At one time, he had amassed a small POW fortune consisting of an American $20 bill, 26 Filipino pesos, $250 in Japanese printed pesos (which the POW's called "Mickey Mouse money" because it was printed in the back of a truck in camp) and two jars of salt. Other POW's came to John all the time to trade for something he had.

John kept his quan in a small gunnysack (canvas bag) which he tied shut with a piece of clothesline and hung it up on the rafters to keep it away from animals, as well as from other POW's. Sergeant Sullivan, who was in his 50's and whose nickname was "Sully," was in charge of the barracks. He would always stay back when the men went out to work details. Sully was supposed to watch John's bag for him in return for a little quan.

John was detailed to work as a "squee-gee" for the Japanese at the Mac Tan rice paddies. He was told by one of the guards to go chop some firewood. Once he had started to chop the wood, the guard left him alone. As he continued to chop and split the wood, he noticed a chicken egg near the woodpile. The Japanese had chickens running all around the area, and finding an egg was like finding a piece of gold. As he looked at the egg, all sorts of things started to run through his mind. What if I get caught? What would these Jap bastards do to me? He calmed down and carefully moved the egg over to a spot where it wouldn't be damaged. He continued chopping, and then found another one. Now John was really excited. How the hell am I gonna get these two eggs back to the compound without getting caught, he thought.

The Japanese guards had issued all the prisoners underwear that the POW's called "G strings." The "G String" was simply a cloth measuring about two feet long and about one foot wide and it had two strings on the end. The POW's tied the strings around their waists. From the back, they would bring the cloth up to the front under the strings, and then drape it over the front of their loins. That way, it covered their front and their rear ends. John made sure his "G-string" was secured.

After his work detail was finished, he placed the two eggs ever so carefully in his crotch area. (He was also wearing cut-off denim pants over the "G-string"). He had to be very careful walking, as well as getting on and off the train that took the POW's back to the compound.

As the prisoners got off the train at the compound, John walked very carefully past the guards who were counting off the prisoners. After passing through the gates, John headed for the hospital to see his friend Major George Hart. The major was one of the few people in camp that John liked and trusted one hundred percent. He was only about 5 feet 6 inches tall, but he was a giant in courage. He had a rather large head and clear blue eyes. He was very smart, and John was glad to know him. Major Hart had been captured on Corregidor, and the Japanese had beaten him so badly that they had damaged his kidneys. Now, at Davao, he was having an operation and was in the camp hospital.

The Major saw John coming and as he got closer, John yelled out, "Hey, Major, I've got something for you." Without another word, John began dropping his shorts. The guys in the Bioki were looking at John, wondering what the hell he was up to. John reached into his crotch and brought out the eggs, one at a time. Major Hart was startled at the sight of a man taking eggs out of his crotch, but when he saw them, he started crying and laughing at the same time.

Then speaking very softly, he said, "John, you surprised the hell out of me. I have received many gifts in my life, but never from that source. Thank you."

"You're welcome, Major. I hope you enjoy your breakfast tomorrow morning," John said.

"John, there are only two people I want to know when this is over. One is Captain Reynolds, and the other is you. You're an honest guy who helps other guys out without expecting anything in return. Unfortunately, most of the other guys aren't like that." The Major saw the puzzled look on John's face, so he added, "You know, John, I have very powerful connections back in the States, and a lot of other guys in camp know that. Sometimes, I suspect that's one of the reasons they're nice to me."

"I don't care who you are. All I know is you're a regular guy," John replied.

"There's a lot of hypocrites out there, John. You can come and visit me any time you want. I enjoy your company."

169

"I know, Major, that we come from different sides of town. I don't have much education or money, and you're a college graduate and come from the upper class," John said.

"That's what I like about you, John. What you see is what you get. Why the heck did you bring me the eggs?" the Major asked.

"That's the way I was brought up. When I was a kid in Brooklyn, my mother would always take a bag of buns with her when she went visiting. I guess it was a kind of Polish tradition," John said.

"And a good tradition it is," Major Hart said. It had become obvious that the major was getting tired, so John told him he had to get back to his barracks and wash up for dinner. The two had quite a few conversations during their stay at Davao, and John considered that meeting and knowing the major was one of the greatest gifts he had ever received in life.

It was a normal practice for two prisoners to team up as "quan partners," not only to share whatever was brought in, but also to protect what they had. Some days, one of the partners would get on a detail that would allow him to bring in some quan, and on other days the buddy would get the detail that allowed him to bring in something. If a POW were to work alone, the number of days that he could bring home some fruit might be few or far between.

John teamed up with a fellow prisoner from Detroit, Julian "Julie" Slimak. John was beginning to have poor eyesight as a result of the bad diet. While on a work detail one day, Slimak pointed over to the woods and asked John, "Do you see that ripe papaya over there?"

"No. What are you talking about?"

"The one with the bright orange-yellow color."

"No, I don't see anything like that. They all look the same to me," John replied.

"Watch the guard. When he turns, let me know," Slimak said. When the guard turned away, John gave Slimak the signal. Slimak chopped the papaya down with his hoe, picked it up and hid behind a tree, where he cut the papaya in half and ate it. Then he came back and told John, "Go ahead. Go over and eat the other half. I'll keep an eye out for you." When the guard turned away again, John went over, picked up the fruit and ate it.

John and Slimak were doing pretty well as quan partners. One time, John shared with Slimak a whole pineapple that he found lying on the ground. It was bright yellow, had a very strong aroma and was very ripe. When John first cut it over his mess kit, the juice ran out into the plate.

Stealing had become a way of life for many POW's. Unfortunately, some of them were not only stealing from the Japanese, but also from their fellow POW's. John and his partner noticed that some of their vegetables and fruits were missing from their small garden. They made some inquiries and found out who the thief was. After "tinko," (evening roll call) Slimak found the guy walking between barracks #6 and #7 and confronted him. Unfortunately for Slimak, the thief was also an amateur boxing champion in the Army. There was a fight, and Slimak was getting the worst of it. When John arrived, he saw his partner lying on the ground with a bloody nose and breathing very hard. John looked at Slimak and said, "What's going on?"

"He's the guy that stole our food," Slimak replied.

"You've had enough. I'll take it from here," John told him.

171

"No. I'll handle him," Slimak told John as he rose on wobbly legs.

"I said, I'll handle him," John repeated.

The thief looked at John and said, "I just cleaned his clock and I'll do the same to you."

John didn't say anything. As they squared off, someone yelled out that the guy was supposed to have been the boxing champion of his weight class in the regular Army.

"I don't care who the hell this guy is. All I know is that he's a thief."

The fight lasted for quite a while, with both men giving and taking some good shots. Finally, John hit him with a right cross to his chest, just above his heart, and the thief fell to the ground and moaned. The fight was over.

"If I ever catch you near our garden again, I'll kill you," John said as he and Slimak left.

"Where the hell did you learn to fight like that?" Slimak asked.

"Greenpoint, Brooklyn," John replied.

The Japanese had given the POW's seeds for white radishes and a type of "peach eye" romaine lettuce, and John had a very nice little crop going. The Japanese did this at a time when they were cutting the rice rations back again. Most of the vegetables were eventually taken by the Japanese to feed their own troops, but the POW's were allowed to keep some.

John noticed that someone was picking vegetables from his little garden. He asked Slimak if he was doing it and Slimak told him he wasn't. But John was suspicious and asked another POW to keep an eye on the garden, in return for some quan. The partnership with Slimak, which had worked quite well for some time, started to crumble after the POW told John that he had seen Slimak picking vegetables from John's 3 by 8 foot garden and selling them so he could play cards. John confronted his quan partner, "Did you take anything out of my garden?"

"No. Why? Did someone say I did?" Slimak replied.

"Someone saw you taking the stuff out," John added. John was going to hit him, but he decided not to. Slimak had helped John once, and he felt he owed him.

"Don't tell me you didn't do it. I know you did it. What I want to know is why you did it."

"I owed some guys money from playing cards. I'm sorry, John," Slimak said.

"I'm sorry too! From now on, stay the hell out of my garden. If I catch you near it again, I'll knock you on your ass."

In early February of 1943, the POW's learned through their short-wave radios that on February 7, 1943, the Japanese had surrendered on Guadalcanal. When the Japanese began to cut their rations even more, the POW's knew that the war was not going well for them. Another good sign was that the POW's would see large numbers of Japanese bombers going south, but rarely saw any come back. Some of the POW's began yelling out a slogan, "The Golden Gate in 48."

One day, John was asked to participate in the beating of a fellow POW. A young Mexican-American from New Mexico had stolen a pair of shoes from a sick POW. He was caught after someone saw him throw the shoes into the latrine. He was not turned over to the Japanese, but he was made to go down into the crap and get the shoes out. The Americans issued the punishment. All of the men from the barracks would be lined up in two rows, and the young man would be forced to walk between them. The other POW's were told to hit him with anything they could find as he passed by them. He was punched, slapped, hit with web belts and other objects. When he came to where John was standing in the line, he was almost in tears, and John did not hit him. The man standing next to John seemed to be very angry and asked, "Why the hell didn't you take a shot at that low-life bastard?"

"I didn't feel like it."

"Why not?" the guy asked.

"None of us here are innocent of stealing. I think he's been punished enough. He has to live with what he did," John answered.

The POW's were always plotting how to get their quan back into the compound. They would take anything that wasn't nailed down, even if they couldn't use it. It could always be used to exchange for something else. There was one prisoner who worked in the rice bodega who had developed a unique system for smuggling rice back into the camp, and every Sunday he would cook an extra portion of rice for himself.

All of the POW's were wearing some sort of "poor man's slipper" – a sandal made out of wood and canvas, which the men called "skivvies." One of the POW's, named Fitzgerald, made a pair of skivvies with high heels. He hollowed out the heels and made a slide to cover the hollowed-out part. It worked pretty well until one day, after being counted off to go into the compound, he was walking across the railroad tracks towards the main gate when the heel broke off and rice spilled out. When the guard saw this, he grabbed Fitzgerald by his long reddish beard and yanked him back and forth. It was actually very funny to see. The other prisoners all laughed, as did the Japanese guards. That was his only punishment. But the next day, there were no more long beards. The prisoners realized that beards made them more vulnerable to the guards.

Guys who were caught smuggling food back into the camp were always beaten, sometimes with fists and sometimes with whatever the guards had in their hands. Lieutenant Hasimoto, "Little Caesar," liked to use the flat side of his sword. One POW was made to stand in a pan of water while the Japanese guards charged it with electricity. John later asked that POW how it felt, and the guy refused to talk about it. John assumed that the guy was scared to death.

Some of the guys who had come up from Del Monte had brought mosquito nets with them, which they placed over their sleeping area. The camp was infested with lice and the lice would often cover the mosquito nets. Rather than pick the lice off, the POW's would place the nets over an ant hill, stir up the hill with a stick, and watch the ants attack and eat the lice.

There were several escapes from Camp Davao. In one incident, nine officers and one enlisted man escaped. They were the first Americans to tell the outside world what the Japanese had done to the American POW's on Bataan and Corregidor. Two other POW's, named Peace and Brown, escaped during a monsoon, but Colonel Olson somehow managed to convince the Japanese that they had drowned in a nearby river during the storm. The Japanese must have bought it, because no one was executed. Another time, a Filipino former convict chopped a Japanese guard's head off and escaped. He took the guard's shoes, rifle and ammo belt.

175

One day, John was walking between two barracks when he saw Lieutenant Donald H. Wills roasting some meat over a charcoal fire. The lieutenant had been in charge of the 26th Filipino Calvary before he was captured. As John got closer, the lieutenant asked, "Hey, Mackowski. Do you want a piece of meat?"

"Yeah, OK." John didn't know what he was cooking, but he decided to try it anyway.

"This tastes pretty good. What is it?"

"Snake," the lieutenant replied.

"Did you say 'snake'?" John asked.

"Yeah. Snake. How does it taste?" Lt. Wills asked.

"Not bad."

"Do you want another piece?"

"No thanks. I got to be going. Thanks again. Leu."

That was the beginning of a rather brief acquaintance. Sometime later, Lieutenant Wills asked John if he was interested in trying to escape with him. Lieutenant Wills knew that John was tough enough to make it to the guerillas once they got away from the camp. He also knew that John had some salt and some money put aside.

John said he was interested, and they devised a plan. During one of their work details, feeding the carp in a pond next to the bodega, they planned to knock the guard out, throw him in the pond, take his rifle and ammo and "head for the hills." Somehow, a POW captain found out about the escape plan and told Colonel Olson, the American commander of the compound, who separated John and Lieutenant Wills. A few days later, John saw this captain in the compound. He stood near him and said loudly enough so everyone could hear, "There's a lot of chicken-shit bastards around here." The captain looked at John, but said nothing.

There was an Italian-American POW from Chicago who got into some trouble with his fellow prisoners. While working in the Japanese kitchen, he was trying to win some special favors from the guard. He was telling the guard, "You know that your ToJo, Hitler and Mussolini are all the 'same-o,' and because I'm an Italian, we're 'cumadachis,' or comrades."

Unfortunately for him, a POW from Texas, Tex Arnold was standing on the other side of a partition. He overheard the conversation, got really ticked off and told everybody what the guy had said. For weeks and weeks, nobody talked to this guy. It got so bad, he went crying to Colonel Olson that no one would talk to him. The colonel just told him that he couldn't order anyone to talk to him if they didn't want to.

And so it went in the daily lives of the POW's at Camp Davao until January and February of 1944 when a rumor began circulating that a large group of POW's would be moved out. On March 1, 1944, the POW's were told that they would be moving out the next day. The men decided to put on an informal show in the compound that night — juggling acts, hillbilly ballads and even comedy routines. Some of the prisoners had rigged up a backdrop out of an old shelter-half tacked to the wall of the church/recreation building, and the performers stood in front of it and sang.

After a while, the Japanese guards wandered away from the barbed wire, bored with a show in the English language. When they had gone, the master of ceremonies held up his hand and in silence pulled aside the shelter-half. And there it was. The men hadn't seen an American flag in two years. It was just a small flag, torn and faded, and the red and white stripes had run together with the rain, but something happened inside of the men as they stood silently and looked at it. They all stood at attention, and in a whisper they all sang "The Star Spangled Banner." There were a thousand men in that compound and they all sang almost without sound. The words passed over their lips like a silent prayer. The only sound that could be heard was when one of the men began to cry.

The next morning, March 2, 1944, 750 prisoners were told that they would be leaving Davao. Most of them, about 650, would be going to a place called Lasang, and the other 100, including John's friend Elmer Searle, would be going to a lumber detail. The conditions had been deplorable in all of the prisoner of war camps that John had been in, but nothing had prepared him for what he was about to experience.

Chapter 8

LASANG
March 1944

The prisoners walked the 10 miles or so from Davao to Lasang, which was located north of Davao on the coast. Their belongings had been sent ahead of them on a couple of trucks. This time, John made sure he was one of the first POW's to get his things off of the truck.

The new camp was dirtier and even more cramped than Davao. The drinking and bathing water came from artesian wells that, unfortunately, were located not too far from the slit trench, which served as the POW's latrine. The camp was ringed with barbed wire strung on 2x4 wooden stakes. Outside, and just to the right of the main gate was the guardhouse, with the bodega still further to the right. The barracks for the guards was also located outside of the barbed-wire-enclosed area. Inside the main compound were four large nipa buildings with thatched roofs. Three of the buildings were used as barracks, and one was used to house the POW kitchen.

On April 29, 1944, the day of the Emperor's birthday, the POWs were made to bow at the waist in his honor. Most of the guys were saying things under their breath as the guards were making them bow; things like, "Up your ass," and "Screw your emperor."

It was starting to become obvious to the POW's that the Japanese were losing the war. Twice during their stay at this camp, the men could hear the drone of planes in the distance and the dull thud of bombs falling. It boosted the morale of the POW's. They knew that the Americans were coming to rescue them, and it didn't seem like the Japanese could stop them.

The guards were becoming extremely violent towards the prisoners. Every day, prisoners were beaten and the rations reduced. Many times, while working at Lasang Airfield, John witnessed the Japanese guards take a POW out of line to beat and torture him. The guards would shove the POW's head into a five-gallon can full of water, hold his head down for 30 seconds or so and then release him. When the man came up gasping for air, one of the guards would punch him in the stomach. Then they would laugh.

One of the men who had been beaten in this fashion was Private Robinson from Seattle, Washington, who was a regular Army man with the 31st Infantry Division. Another fellow was named Hall. He was with the 200th Coast Artillery, a New Mexico outfit. Robinson and Hall said they were questioned about plans the POW's might have for escape.

In early July, the men saw a dark cloud in the sky. At first, they couldn't figure out what it was, but it was heading right for the camp. Then they heard the sound of insects flying all around them. They were now soon under siege by a large army of locusts. There were so many of them that when Japanese trucks and tanks ran over them the men could hear a crunching sound.

During this "plague of locusts," John saw one of the strangest things he would ever see as a POW. Two American quan partners inside the compound were running around with a mosquito net in the air. Each was holding onto one end of the net and they were catching the locusts. By the time they had run around the compound, they had caught quite a few of them. They pulled the heads off the locusts and fried them using Barbasol shaving cream (which contained peanut oil), that they had received earlier in a Red Cross package. John walked over to the two men as they sat eating locusts and asked, "How the hell can you eat those things?"

"You dumb Polack," one of the guys replied. "Didn't you ever read your Bible. The Jews ate them when they had a plague of locusts, so we're eating them now."

"What do they taste like?"

"You want to find out?" one of them asked.

"No. I just want to know what they taste like."

"They taste like shrimp. You can have one if you like."

"No thanks. Not today." John replied.

Red Cross packages came twice during John's stay in the prison camps, but the Japanese guards usually kept most of the items. When the first packages came to Davao in 1943, they contained shoes that were initially given to the POW's, but later confiscated by the guards in order to prevent escapes.

Lieutenant Hoshidai (Bulbnose) and Lieutenant Hashimoto (Little Cesear) had also come to Lasang and were in charge. Lieutenant Hoshidai was the camp commander. He had been a schoolteacher in civilian life. He was in his mid-thirties, wore a mustache and spoke very good English. Second in command was Lieutenant Hashimoto, who had come up through the ranks. He was about 25 years old, 5'2" tall and wore tortoise-shell glasses. He was built like a little wrestler, with a bull neck and short thick legs. The American POW doctor at the camp said that Little Caesar had a bad case of syphilis and it was affecting his thinking, causing extreme mood swings.

One day, while John was working in the POW kitchen, a Japanese guard went over to Captain Wexler, the American officer in charge of the kitchen, and told him he needed two POW's. Captain Wexler told John and another POW, John White, to go over to the guard and do what he wanted. When they did, the guard said in broken English, "You two must go on detail and kill pig. Go! Speedo! Speedo!"

As the two men walked out of the kitchen towards a small platform near the well, John thought, What the hell do I know about killing a goddamn pig? I hope someone knows what he's doing.

John White saw the apprehensive look on John's face and said, "Don't look so worried, city boy. I've done this a hundred times back home in Montana." White killed the small, sixty-pound pig by tying its legs together, putting his foot on the pigs head and slitting its throat. The POW's in the camp had strings of pork in their rice that night.

On another occasion, four POW's, including John Mackowski and John White, were told to go with a Japanese guard to kill a caribou. The group went out of the compound, past the bodega, to a spot near the river. One of the men walked up to the caribou who was busy grazing on the lush grass and tied a heavy rope around the twelve-hundred-pound animal's horns. They somehow managed to wrap the rope around a tree so he couldn't move. The guard gave John White an axe. White hit the caribou on the head with the blunt side. The animal struggled fiercely to get free. It was kicking and grunting so hard that it looked for a moment like it was going to break the rope that was holding it. When the guard and the POW's saw what was happening, they took off running in the direction of the camp. John picked up the axe and lifted it high in the air. Using the sharp edge this time, he brought it down with all of the strength he could muster and hit the animal square on the head. It fell down dead with its legs spread out. John White cut the animal up and let the stomach float down the river so the natives could find it and eat it. A POW veterinarian sliced up the liver, but seeing that it was filled with parasites, he threw it away. The POW's got to keep the front part of the animal, and the guards got the rest.

Late one afternoon around dusk, the men saw a small Japanese commuter-type plane with twin engines flying in circles around the airstrip. It looked like one of the wheels in the landing gear was stuck in the retracted position. The pilot kept circling the airfield, apparently trying to burn up his fuel.

When he finally decided to land, the pilot flew over the camp at about 100 feet or so over the trees and headed towards the airfield. The men couldn't see what happened to the plane, but they all heard a loud crash. Most of the POW's just looked at each other and smiled. One guy yelled out, "That's one son-of-a-bitch that won't be flying anymore!" The guards were very sore at the prisoners for smiling, but they didn't do anything because they were outside the compound.

Chapter 9

AN ATROCITY
August 1944

Captain Wetzel was ordered to put a detail together to get rations from the bodega. Ten men were assigned in two-man teams. Each team was to carry one rice basket full of tangkong, a green leafy vegetable. The baskets were about 2 1/2 feet in diameter and about 1 1/2 feet deep. In order to carry the large baskets, a bamboo pole was inserted through the loops on both ends of the basket. Each man would take one end of the pole and place it on his shoulder. John was teamed up with a prisoner named Jack, whom he hardly knew. Other POW's on this detail were S/Sgt. Hayes H. Bolitho of Montana, S/Sgt. Peter J. Golino, Privates Isaac B. Hagins, John White, Raymond Rebouche, Bradley and Harlan.

As they were loading up the baskets at around 11:00 AM, another prisoner placed a pair of tin-snips into John and Jack's basket. [This POW's real name is not used for obvious reasons. A fake nickname, "Macko" will be used to identify him henceforth.] Jack didn't see the other POW do this, but John did. He told Macko, "Get them fucking things out of our basket."

"Don't worry, they won't find it," Macko replied.

Jack looked at John, wondering what he was talking to Macko about. John felt that Macko had really put him and Jack on the spot. If John said or did anything to expose Macko, the POW's would call him a squealer, a rat and/or any other number of names. On the other hand, John and Jack would have to face the punishment if the guards found the tin-snips in their basket.

The group headed back to the camp. Of the five teams, John and Jack were the fourth in line. After walking about 200 feet or so carrying the tangkong, the group was ordered to stop. John turned to Macko, who was behind him, and said, "There's going to be a showdown. If we get caught, you'd better own up to it."

The guard walked down the line. He did not search the first, second or third baskets, but went directly to John and Jack's basket, the fourth in line. He reached down into the area where the tin-snips had been placed, pulled them out and then called for the corporal. When the guard showed the corporal the tin snips, the corporal ordered the detail to go back to the compound.

When they arrived back at the compound, John told Macko, "I don't give a shit what you tell them, but you better tell them Jap guards that you put them tin snips in our basket. Otherwise, we're all going to get punished."

"Don't worry. Nothing's gonna' happen," Macko said.

Macko was in the Navy. His P.T. boat had been badly damaged when it attacked a Japanese cruiser around Cebu. There were two other crewmen from the same P.T. boat in the camp — James Light and a fellow called "Ike," short for Ikelberger.

Around four or five o'clock in the afternoon, the ten POW's were ordered to go to the guardhouse. The guardhouse was a 20 foot by 40 foot wooden building with a corrugated tin roof and a small covered step-up porch on the front. There was a small table and a couple of chairs on the porch where the guards used to sit and watch the prisoners.

The men were formed up in two lines of five. John was in the front row, the second from the left. Macko was also in the first row, at the other end. Facing the group was Lieutenant Hashimoto, "Little Caesar," who seemed to be growing more and more irrational every day. He would fly into violent fits of rage at the slightest provocation, then repent and try to make amends. He was drinking a lot, and at times would go out of his mind completely. It was not a good time for a POW to get in trouble. Speaking through an interpreter, Lieutenant Hashimoto called out once, "Who is the guilty person?" No one responded. Little Caesar called out again in Japanese, and the interpreter repeated, "I said, who is the guilty person?" Again, no one responded or moved. Then, looking straight at Macko, Lieutenant Hashimoto spoke in Japanese and the interpreter said, "I'm going to call out once more, and if the guilty person does not admit the theft, you are all going to be punished in the guardhouse."

John thought, Hashimoto knows that Macko took the tin-snips. John glanced to the right where, Macko was standing, hoping that he would move forward. But he didn't. He seemed to be frozen in place. John could hear the grumbling of the other POW's behind him, "Why don't you own up to it, Mackowski." "We're all gonna get it now because of you." "Come on John. Tell 'em you did it."

John realized that most of the POW's standing in line thought that he had stolen the tin-snips. John was caught in a "Catch-22" situation. If he told on Macko, he would be branded a squealer. If he said nothing, the whole group would be punished.

He thought of the situation that faced another POW at another camp. That POW had decided to yell out to the Japanese guards when he saw two prisoners trying to escape. That POW had also been caught in the middle of a no-win situation. If the prisoners had escaped, ten POWs would have been killed in retaliation. (In this camp, the Japanese would kill five POWs for every one that escaped.) The two escapees were caught and executed. The POW who yelled out had to live with his decision. He definitely had caused the death of the two POW's trying to escape, but he also saved the lives of ten other POW's who would have surely been killed if the escape had been successful.

Lt. Hashimoto began to speak again in Japanese, and the interpreter also began to speak, "This is the last time, I... ." Before he could finish his sentence, John told the interpreter, "Tell him that I put the tin snips in the basket."

As the interpreter spoke to the Japanese lieutenant, John looked directly into the lieutenant's face. The lieutenant's mouth opened wide with amazement, and he once again glanced over in Macko's direction. He knew that Macko had stolen the tin snips.

The Japanese loved to plant all sorts of things around that would look good to the Americans. They would watch until one of the POW's took the item, then they would "catch" the thief and beat the stuffing out of him. For the guards, it served one main purpose: it showed the prisoners that they were in charge. It worked, most of the time, because it kept the prisoners in a constant state of fear and uncertainty.

Lieutenant Hashimoto motioned with his right arm for John to step out of line and go to the front of the guardhouse. The other nine Americans, including Macko, were sent back to the compound. John's hands were tied behind him and he was taken to the bodega. Little Caesar and five guards surrounded John and took turns beating him when he wouldn't tell them why the tin-snips were in his basket or who was trying to escape with him. They passed him around the ring and beat him until he fell. He would then be picked up, revived and beaten again. When they realized he wasn't going to talk, he was taken back to the guardhouse.

Once inside the guardhouse, he was placed in his new "quarters," a small cage. The cage consisted of wooden 2 x 4's about six inches apart going from the floor to the roof, which was made of corrugated metal. There was a small two-foot by two-foot opening at the lower right end for entering and exiting, which was secured with a padlock. The floor was made from wide boards. There was a small wooden box in the corner for a toilet.

The guards made him take off all his clothes and pass them out to them between the wooden bars. That first night was the coldest that John could ever remember in the Philippines. He was completely nude. At first, he tried to keep warm by encircling his arms around his body. Then, the guards forced him to stand at attention. He was not allowed to lie down or sit. One guard that first night kept staring at John's penis and calling him "caribou." The only thing John still had with him was a button from his shirt, which he had hidden in his mouth. He didn't know why he kept it. It had fallen off when he was taking his clothes off and he decided to keep it.

The next morning, John was given his shorts back, but he was forced to continue to stand at attention. Around 10:30 AM, the guards came and took him to the headquarters building where he appeared before a group of Japanese officers. The senior lieutenant in charge, Hoshidai, quickly pronounced his sentence through an interpreter, "You were caught stealing. You admitted the crime and now you are going to be punished. You will serve twenty-one days of solitary confinement in the guardhouse." (The Japanese actually added an extra day. The sentencing did not take place until the day after John had already served one day.) John's rations were cut to one-half a canteen cup full of water a day, plus a small portion of rice about the size of a leveled-off can of Del Monte tomato herrings.

During those first days, he was never allowed to move or even sit down without permission. When not standing, he was forced to sit on his haunches, which cut off blood circulation in his legs. They started to swell all the way up to his hips. Although the guard would change, John was still made to stand at attention. If he moved without permission, he would be hit over the head with a metal rod. In the evenings, he received his small ration of water and rice.

The Japanese guards assigned to watch John were as different from one another as night is from day. Many of the guards had mixed features and didn't look like they were 100% Japanese. A few of the guards were particularly mean. They would sometimes dump John's meager rations on the floor and give him very little water. One guard handed John a cigarette and told him to chew it. Chewing the cigarette made him pretty sick, but John refused to show it. He actually smiled at the guard while he ate it. One Japanese corporal came in a few times, pointed at John and said, "Genkee," which means "strong." There were some good Japanese guards also. One gave John some of his water and allowed him to walk around in his small cell and sit on the little wooden crate that served as a seat. He would ask John if he was "okaga," slang for "OK."

John had quite a few Japanese officers visiting him on a regular basis. After one of these visits, one guard gave John a good tongue-lashing because the officer had told him that John looked too strong. The guard wanted John to look more beaten and weak when the officers came. The guard was afraid he would get in trouble if John didn't look in bad shape. So John and the guard had a special arrangement. When the guard hit the butt of his rifle on the floor, John would stand at attention immediately and look like he was in pain.

While confined to his cage, John had a daily visit from a mouse. It would run from one end of the cell to the other. It was the only living thing, other than the Japanese guards, that John would see for twenty-two days. One day, a particularly odd-looking guard caught the mouse and took quite a bit of pleasure stroking its underside and pinching its nipples. Finally, the guard twisted its head and threw it out the window. John was mad as hell. It had been the only thing he looked forward to seeing every day, and now it, too, was gone.

While John was confined in his cage in the guardhouse, Private Raymond Rebouche was on a work detail when he spotted a candy bar on a table at the bodega. He put it in his basket. It was evidently a trap set by the guards. A few moments later, one of the guards, a two-star private named Okomoto, whose only distinctive feature was a lot of gold showing in his teeth, went over to the table and saw that the candy bar was missing. He began to search all the baskets.

Private Rebouche told the guard that he had taken the candy, and was immediately struck along the side of his head with the butt of the guard's rifle, knocking him to his knees. Then he was kicked in the groin and hit again with the rifle. He and Captain Wetzel were taken outside, and 2x4's were placed behind their knees. They were forced to squat down on their feet with the 2x4's behind their knees and hold another 2x4 over their heads. Every time they moved forward to ease the pressure on their legs, or lower their arms to rest for a moment, they were punched in the face or struck with a rifle butt.

Back in his cage, the days were passing very slowly for John. One guard kept tormenting him by telling him that he was going to die. The guard kept saying "bati," which in Japanese means "to die." John told him in broken Japanese, "All ostas nippon bati. American scogi (airplane) pom-pom all nippon bati."

This went on for quite a while. The guard would hit John with a long rod, and John would laugh at him. And so it went, on and on. John always took his time eating because it was the only time the guards would leave him alone and he could rest. He ate his rice one-grain at a time in order to stall for time. On one occasion, he counted out 203 grains of rice in his cup. A few times, he noticed that his rice was yellow. He hoped that the guards hadn't urinated in the rice, but he was starving. He had no choice but to eat it anyway.

Whenever his fellow POWs would pass by the guardhouse, John could hear words of encouragement from them, "Don't let them get to you." "Hang in there, kid." "We're behind you."

One POW from New Jersey, Alex Karpeski, who was also of Polish descent, shouted out in Polish, "Show them sons-of-bitches what we Poles are made of. Stand proud." Karpeski was from Company B of the 803rd Aviation Engineers. Later, the Japanese permitted only silence as the POW's passed by.

John was starting to wonder why he had to endure this torture. He thought that he had been chosen by God to endure this punishment for past sins. Maybe, he thought, I'm just going crazy!

Around the ninth day, a short Japanese guard who looked like a monkey and whose nickname was 'Mickey Mouse' started off with the usual treatment. He made John stand at attention for quite a long time. Then he made him sit on his haunches for what seemed like an even longer period of time. It was becoming very painful. Finally, John could no longer sit in this position and he rolled over onto the floor of the cage. "Mickey Mouse" became enraged and started to shout at John in Japanese, but John couldn't understand what he was saying. Another guard came in and started arguing with the first guard. He was telling him, more or less, to give John a break and let him stand up. As the other guard was leaving the room, John finally managed to pull himself up by grabbing onto the wooden 2x4's.

When "Mickey Mouse" saw that John had somehow managed to stand up, he began yelling at him again in Japanese. John didn't understand what the guard was saying, but he saw that the guard was now pointing a rifle with a fixed bayonet at him. The guard kept jabbing at John with the bayonet through the openings in the wooden slats. Each time, he was getting closer and closer. John timed his moves, and the next time the guard jabbed at him, John side-stepped and, with all of his might, pulled the rifle from the guard smashing him up against the wooden slats of the cage. John stood there with the rifle in his hands. What the hell do I do now? John wondered. Here I am in a cage, holding a Jap guard's rifle. How the hell am I gonna get out of this one?

The two just stood there and looked at each other for a few seconds, each just as surprised as the other. It was a very unique situation. Inside of the cage, with no hope of getting out, was a POW holding a rifle. Outside of the cage was a guard, who had just been disarmed by a prisoner. The guard yelled out in Japanese and two other guards quickly came through the front of the building. They looked at "Mickey Mouse," and then they looked at John, who was standing there inside the cell holding the guard's rifle. There was a lot more shouting in Japanese, and finally one of the guards left. A minute or so later, the other guard and Lieutenant Hashimoto came in. When John saw the lieutenant, he said, "That son-of-a-bitch is a no good bastard. He was trying to stick me with his pig sticker, and I just couldn't take any more of it."

Lt. Hashimoto said nothing, nor did he have to say anything. He simply put his hand on his gun, and John passed the guard's rifle through the wooden bars of his cage, butt first. The Lieutenant looked at "Mickey Mouse" and started to yell at him. When the guard answered, the lieutenant began to beat the guard, punching and slapping his face.

Then, Lieutenant Hashimoto took off his gun belt, picked up the flap to the cage and made a motion like he was going to come in and give John a judo lesson. John looked the lieutenant straight in the eye and said, "Come on in and try me, if you think you're man enough! I'll beat the shit out of you!" John yelled out as loud as he could, "Come on! Come on! I don't care anymore if I die! You're going to kill me anyway! Let's get it over with!"

Hashimoto ordered John to turn around, back up to the wooden slats of the cage and extend his arms in the open position. As he complied, each arm was tied to the slats. Then he was told to stand on his tiptoes with his heels up. Then, his legs were tied to the wooden slats about one foot apart, leaving his knees in the bent position. If he moved, a guard would hit him over the head with a metal rod. The pain was unbearable, which caused him to move many times. Each time he moved, he would be struck again. His arms and legs became swollen and started to become numb.

Over the next few days, the guards came in many times and gave John severe beatings. He began to have a hard time seeing because his eyes were so swollen from the beatings. John was now beginning to think that it was just about all over for him. He was sure that the guards had been ordered to beat him until he died. Each time they came in, he thought, "this is it." He said his prayers to himself and was prepared to die. There's nothing more these bastards can do to me because I am no longer afraid of death, he thought, as he heard the guards coming in the cage.

The guards began their usual ritual. They yelled at him in Japanese and started to hit him with their fists and a metal rod. When he slumped down, they kicked him with their boots. There came a point when John just couldn't feel the pain any more. He knew the guards were hitting him because he could feel the impact of their blows, but he just couldn't feel the pain. As he felt himself slipping away from the reality of a very cruel world, he managed to somehow muster the strength to show his captors one last act of defiance. It was just a faint smile, but it would show them that in spite of what they had done to him, they hadn't defeated him.

Just before he was beaten into unconsciousness, he yelled out loud, "For all the things I may have done wrong, God, I hope this evens the score a little." He said a few more prayers to himself because he felt that death was closing in. Then he passed out. Seeing that he was unconscious, the guards cut the ropes and John fell to the floor of his cage bleeding and barely breathing.

The next thing John remembered was waking and finding himself lying on the floor of his cage. He thought to himself: God! I can't believe I'm still alive! As he stirred slowly, he heard the Japanese guard shouting and banging his rifle on the floor. He thought that the guards would surely be coming in now to finish him off.

But the guard standing outside the cage was one of the good guards. He had a broad smile on his face and actually looked happy to see that John was still alive. Just then, another guard came in. The two began talking quickly and appeared to be very excited. John could feel dried, caked blood around his mouth and nose. His eyes were almost swollen shut, but somehow he managed to pull himself up just as Lt. Hashimoto walked in. John had a strange feeling, like he was in limbo.

Lt. Hashimoto spoke to him in perfect English, "Tonight, you will be allowed to sleep. Then he said yasumei (rest) in Japanese. You will receive an extra rice ration and a large quantity of tea." As the Lieutenant spoke, he had a smile on his face that made John suspicious. John thought this had to be the beginning of some new kind of torture.

"You're not giving me another line of bullshit, are you, Lieutenant?" John asked. He noticed two Japanese canteens hanging outside of his cell, and he said to the Lieutenant, "If you're telling me the truth, give me one of those canteens of mizu (water). John pointed to the canteens. Lieutenant Hashimoto smiled and ordered one of the guards to give a canteen to John. He drank it all and asked for the other canteen. It was also given to him.

"Arigato (thank you)," John told the lieutenant. The lieutenant smiled, then turned and left the building. Shortly thereafter, John received the largest, heaping messkit full of rice and tea that he had ever received as a POW. He was also given a blanket and told to "yasumei" (rest). After eating and drinking his fill, he stretched out on the blanket and fell asleep.

The next day was his 22nd day in the cage. After the POW's had left to go to work at the airfield, Lieutenant Hashimoto and three Japanese guards came into the guardhouse. As one of the guards unlocked the small door on the cage, Lieutenant Hashimoto said, "Mackowski, come out here!" John thought to himself that Lieutenant Hashimoto seemed able to pronounce his name better than some of his American sergeants could. It took him a few minutes, but John managed to crawl out of the cage and stand up. One of the guards tied his hands loosely behind his back, and he was marched out of the guardhouse and over to camp headquarters. While en route to camp headquarters, he stumbled and fell a few times, but each time he fell the guards patiently waited for him to upright himself. John hadn't walked for 22 days and the guards allowed him to set his own pace.

He was taken into the headquarters building and stood before the prison camp commander, Lieutenant Hoshidai. Lt. Hoshidai said through a Filipino interpreter, "We know you shielded another American, and we know who he is. You paid the penalty for a crime that you did not commit, and we admire you as a professional soldier."

"Tell the lieutenant that I'm not a professional soldier," John responded through the interpreter.

"I don't understand," the lieutenant replied.

"President Roosevelt sent me a letter, and I came," John said. Upon hearing his reply, the Japanese officers and guards laughed.

"If you tell anyone what we did to you, we will kill you," the lieutenant said.

"What the hell else can you do to me?" John answered.

At that point, Lieutenant Hoshidai waved his hand as if to say, "OK, enough is enough," and John was sent back to the compound. Two guards escorted him back to the gates. Then, he walked by himself back to his barracks. It was a very slow and painful walk, as both his legs were swollen up to his thighs.

John's first visitor was Major Heidger, who was originally from Bridgeport, Connecticut. He was the American POW medical officer, and he told John to get some rest and keep his feet elevated to avoid gangrene setting in.

Lt. Hashimoto came to visit him the next day. Although Hashimoto seemed to be a very cruel person most of the time, occasionally he would show some signs of being a decent human being. He ordered John to follow him to the American POW kitchen. When they got there, he ordered the POW's to heat up some water. He looked at John, who was standing there with short pants and a shirt on, and told him to take his clothes off. Pinching his nose with his fingers, Hashimoto said, "Mackowski, you not only look pretty shitty. You also smell pretty shitty." Then he ordered two American Kp's on duty at the time, John White and Peter Galino, to wash John. A day or two later, Lieutenant Hashimoto visited John in the barracks after "tinko." He told the two POWs on either side of John that if John died, they would be killed. To emphasize his point, he took out his sword and pointed it at them. On another occasion, when he was drunk, Hashimoto made the Americans POW's stand at attention inside the barracks while he walked up and down the ranks with John behind him, followed by two Japanese guards. While walking through the lines of American soldiers, he said, "All Americans are bullshit; Mackowski number one hati (soldier)."

Another day, while John was still recovering from the effects of his torture, Hashimoto again came to the barracks to see him. He asked about John's family and told John that he, too, had come from a large family. He had always been a soldier in the Japanese Army, and had fought in Manchuria and other parts of China. It was a strange feeling for John — to chat with the man who had ordered him to be punished so cruelly. And yet, here was the same man showing signs of compassion. Just before he left, Hashimoto handed John a pack of Japanese cigarettes, which the Americans called the "Around the World" brand because the pack had a picture of the sphere of the earth on it.

After a few days of lying with his feet elevated, John received a visit from Macko. He came with a canteen full of Nescafe coffee, which he had received in a Red Cross package. He offered it to John. John spoke first, "Why the hell didn't you own up to it?"

There was silence for a few seconds, then Macko started to cry. "I don't know why I didn't say anything. I guess I was just afraid."

"Don't tell anyone what happened. Let's try to keep it between us," John told him.

All of the anger John had felt towards Macko just melted away. John remembered that he had been afraid many times himself and that Macko had simply been frozen by fear.

One of John's close buddies at Lasang was James Light. He was a tall, well-built Navy PT- man from California who stood about 6'2". He had a big broad smile, a well-trimmed pencil-thin mustache, and he was a good friend to John, who somewhat admired him. John found out that while he was in the cage, Light had gone to Major Heidger and told him that some of the Japanese guards were dumping his rice rations. He asked Major Heiger for some vitamin pills. When he received them, he ground them up and put them in John's rice rations. That's what gave the rice the yellow color from time to time.

Because John was considered an escape risk, he was no longer allowed to go outside the compound on work details. He was usually assigned to chop firewood inside the camp with James Light. Light was after John every day to tell him what really happened. He knew that John didn't put the tin-snips in the basket. He was relentless. He kept after John, day after day. While chopping wood one day, Light asked John, "Come on, Polack, tell me what happened."

"I'm not telling you nothing," John replied.

"Did that yellow bastard have something to do with it?"

"I don't know what you're talking about," John kept saying. Finally, after repeated questioning, John turned to Light and said, "Alright. If you promise to keep your mouth shut, I'll tell you."

"OK Polack, shoot!"

"It was Macko!" John said quietly.

Light banged his axe into a log and said, "I knew it. I knew the yellow bastard had something to do with it."

"You promised me you wouldn't say anything. You promised, and I'm holding you to your promise," John said.

"Don't worry, Polack, I won't tell a soul."

"Thanks. We all make mistakes out here. Let's just say he made a mistake."

"OK! But you're one son-of-a-bitch I want to know when this is over. I don't care where you wind up, I'll find you," Light said.

"Yeah, and I'll lock the door on you if I see you coming," John said with half a laugh.

"And I'll knock it down with a friggin' axe," Light said, as they went back to chopping wood.

One evening, while still recovering from his ordeal in the guardhouse, John was in the barracks preparing to go out for "tinko." He decided to put on a light jacket because it was somewhat cool outside. As he was putting his right arm into the sleeve, he felt a sharp pain like he had just been socked in the jaw. He threw down his jacket and saw a huge scorpion, about 5 or 6 inches long, scurrying under the floorboards. He also saw all sorts of colors. He yelled, "Holy shit! Something bit me!"

One of the other POWs said, "Hey, John, you're bleeding on your right shoulder."

"I think I just got stung by a scorpion. I hope I'm not gonna die from it."

"You better check it out with Heidger," the other POW said.

After standing "tinko," John went to Major Heidger, the POW doctor, who assured him that he wasn't going to die. He gave John some Epsom salts, and told him to rest because he would be very sick for the next day or two as a result of the bite. The major was quite surprised the next morning, however, when he saw John standing in front of him in the chow line.

Major Heidger shook his head from side to side and said, "What the hell are you doing up, Mackowski."

"Excuse me, Major?" John replied.

"You should be very sick."

"It's OK, Major. I feel fine."

"I think you're a lucky man, John," The Major said.

"Lucky? You call getting stung by a scorpion lucky?" John asked.

"The poison must have run out when you were bleeding."

"I don't know anything about that, Major. All I know is that I'm pretty hungry today," John said as they both laughed. He laughed about it that morning, but getting stung by a scorpion was something that John would never forget.

In the beginning of August of 1944, a Catholic chaplain, Father LaFleur, who everybody called "Padre," came over to John and asked him if he would like to join him and a couple of other POW's in saying the rosary. Why is the Padre asking me to come over and pray? John wondered.

"I'll try it, Padre. I'll be over after tinko."

When John got there, he saw only a handful of other POW's kneeling with the padre. The padre was saying some prayers and the small group of men was repeating them. John joined the group and prayed with them for a few days.

A few days later, around dusk, John was reciting prayers with the group. He happened to look up at the sky and noticed that it was starting to get dark. He kept staring at the sky, almost as if he were in a trance. Then, to his surprise, he saw something. In the dark blue sky there was a bright light beginning to appear. He didn't know if he was hallucinating or not, but a face was starting to appear within the light. He was now looking at the face of a thin man with a short beard who very much resembled the face of Jesus that had been etched on his canteen several years earlier. The face was surrounded by a very bright white light, in sharp contrast to the dark blue, darkening sky. As he was repeating the prayers of Father LaFleur, he clearly heard a voice say, "You will return."

John became very scared and got chills all over his body. When the padre finished saying the prayers, he noticed that John was staring at the sky as if in a trance.

"John, are you alright?" the padre asked. He had to shake John a little to get him to come out of his trance-like state.

"Yeah, Padre. I'm fine." With that, the padre gave John a pair of black rosary beads which were probably the last ones that he had.

John received two letters while he was at Lasang. They were the only two he ever received while he was a POW. For some reason, they were both uncensored. Maybe because of what I went through the Japanese guards decided not to censor my mail, John thought. It really didn't matter why they were uncensored, what really mattered was that these two letters were the only mail he had received since the fall of Corregidor.

One was from Opal and contained her picture. He showed the picture to one of his barracks mates, Reuben Gomez from New Mexico.

"She's very beautiful," Gomez said.

"Yeah, ain't she?" John replied.

Then Gomez said, "How was it in there?"

"Where?" John asked.

"In the guardhouse. We could hear them knocking you around quite a bit."

"It was pretty rough and I would rather not talk about it."

"OK. I understand." Gomez changed the conversation back to Opal and he never brought the subject up again.

The other letter John received was from his Uncle Lou. John's uncle wrote, in the context of the family having a meal, "The spaghetti has been eaten. The sauerkraut is being cooked and the rice is being polished."

After reading the letter, John knew that the Italians had surrendered and that the Allies were winning in Europe and in the Pacific. As the letter was passed around the barracks, the men knew that help was on the way — if only their captors didn't kill them before the Americans arrived.

Chapter 10

THE VOYAGE OF THE SHINYO MARU
August-September 1944

In mid-August of 1944, the Japanese began moving the POW's out of Lasang Prison Camp. On the morning of August 20, 1944, as the men stood in formation, about one hundred names were called out. Those who were called were told to go to their barracks, get their possessions and return. After they returned and were all accounted for, the group was marched from the camp. This was repeated several times. Alex Karpeski and Carl Frawling from Company B, 803rd Engineers, left with one of the groups. The number of POW's remaining in John's barracks began to dwindle until, finally, he was the only one left. He began to wonder why he was the only one left. He thought, for sure, that he was going to be killed. His name was finally called, and he was told to get his things and go to the rear of the compound.

He was told he was leaving, but he wasn't told where he would be going. The scuttlebutt among the POW's that morning was that because the Japanese were losing the war, they were taking all of the POW's back to Japan so the Americans wouldn't bomb the home islands. John arrived at the rear of the compound and saw nineteen other POW's standing behind an open truck. On the truck bed was a Japanese guard with a .30 caliber machine gun facing out the back.

A heavy rope had been tied from the left rear of the truck to the right rear of the truck, forming a kind of large "U." A ¾- inch-thick rope was then tied from one side of the rope, laced around the waist of each POW to form a row of five, and then the other end was tied to the other side of the heavy rope. There were three rows of POW's standing behind the truck already secured in this fashion. When John got to the truck, there was a row of four POW's waiting. He would make it five. John put the rope around his waist, and a guard tied the end to the heavier rope. In all, there were twenty POW's tied to the truck. Although John didn't know any of their names, he recognized many of them as POW's who had been slapped around by the guards quite a bit and who were probably considered escape risks, like himself.

This special group of 20 American POW's, tied like water buffaloes behind the truck, walked ten miles to an area on the shore at Davao where they met up with the other POW's who had been taken out of Lasang earlier. Now, the total number of POW's in this group numbered about seven hundred and fifty, including those who had been on the lumber detail.

For quite awhile, the men just stood around on the shore and on the small pier looking out at a transport ship that was anchored about a mile off shore. Then during the afternoon, all 750 men were taken in groups of fifty or so by motorized barges from the small pier on the shoreline to a dilapidated Japanese transport ship, the Erie Maru.

As John climbed up the rope ladder to get on the deck the ship, he saw a Japanese warship anchored nearby. It was either a destroyer or a light cruiser that had obviously seen better days. It was pretty weather-beaten and rusty. All of the POW's were put in the hold of the Erie Maru. The hold contained the remnants, as well as the stench of animal waste. But it was quite large, so the men were able to stretch out a bit on the floor.

The ship remained in the harbor for several days without moving, and the hatch covers were kept open to let air in. Early one morning, the guards suddenly closed the hatch covers. As the ship slowly got underway, the men could hear muffled sounds of explosions and gunfire not too far away.

With the hatches now closed, conditions in the hold deteriorated very rapidly. Within a few minutes, the temperature climbed to well over a hundred degrees. With the heat and the lack of air, many of the men started passing out. They frantically yelled up to the guards to open the hatch covers, but there was no response.

"Lieutenant Hashimoto! Open the hatch! The men are dying down here!" Colonel Rogers called up to anyone who would listen, but there was still no response from the guards. "For God's sake, open the hatches! We need air!" he yelled. Again there was no response. Conditions were getting worse.

At one point, Padre LaFleur stood up and said, "It doesn't look good for us men. I would like everyone to join me in prayer."

Everyone thought for sure, they were all going to die that day. Just about everyone joined the padre in saying the "Our Father." John was becoming very sleepy and drowsy. He felt like he was floating on a cloud. I guess this is it! He thought. It looks like I'm gonna die.

"Padre, please hear my confession," he called out.

"John, I can't do it now. Just say an Act of Contrition and it will be alright," the padre yelled back. Just as John began saying the prayer, the guards opened the hatches and a rush of fresh air came in. One of John's buddies, Alex Karpeski, made some room for him near the hatches, and within a short period of time, John was starting to feel better. Four POWs were hoisted up to the deck that day. They never came back. The men in the hold assumed that they had died.

The Erie Maru continued on its journey, hugging the coast and stopping frequently. There was no rain during the trip, and the men could see the stars at night through the open hatches. They were given one meal a day, which consisted of small amounts of rice and water. The toilet was a five-gallon metal can that was passed around to those who needed it, but because the POWs were hardly given anything to eat or drink during the trip, the can was never filled up. Very few POW's, if any, had a bowel movement that trip and most could only urinate a few drops. They were all becoming dehydrated.

One day, the ship stopped and all the POW's were ordered topside. They were being transferred to another ship, the Shinyo Maru. Down the rope ladder onto a motor launch, up another rope ladder and into the hold of the other ship they went. Once all of the POWs were in the hold, the long ladders were pulled up and the hatch covers were closed. The Shinyo Maru was a lot smaller than the previous ship, and it was filthy. It must have carried cement or some similar cargo fairly recently, because a cement-like powder was all over the floor of the hold. The men were packed in like sardines in a can. They were so close together that one POW would have to stand up in order to allow the person opposite him to stretch his legs a little.

The Japanese guards on this ship were truly rotten. They would send the rice down at the same time they were hauling up the tin of urine and human waste. Many times, they would purposely shake the container containing the waste matter causing some of its contents to spill into the container of rice, as well as onto some of the men below. The ship would move for awhile, and then it would stop for periods of time. Japanese interpreters warned the POW's that if the ship were attacked by allied warplanes, the guards would kill them all.

It was now September 7, 1944. At around 3:20 PM, the U.S.S. Paddle, an American submarine on patrol near Sindangan Point off Mindanao, sighted smoke on the horizon at 242 degrees. By 4:30 PM, the submarine had located the small convoy and was zeroing in on several possible targets, including the Shinyo Maru. At exactly 4:51 PM, the U.S.S. Paddle fired its four bow torpedoes from 1800 or so feet away from the convoy, immediately following those with several other torpedoes aimed at the escort ships.

John was sitting in the forward hold of the Shinyo Maru talking with Al Karpeski, Carl Frawling and Gus Lapinski, all from the 803rd Engineers. They were just passing the time, trying to figure out where the Japanese were taking them, when all of a sudden they heard a loud thundering noise coming from the stern of the ship. The ship began to shake and shudder.

No one in the hold knew what was happening. The Japanese could be heard scurrying around on deck. A bugle could be heard at first, but the notes quickly trailed off, probably because the bugler had become frozen with fear or was trying to save his own life. The POWs were yelling at the guards to let them out. Then, all of a sudden, several guards began firing machine guns and throwing grenades into the hold. The young soldier from Massachusetts, Elmer Searle, called over to John, "Johnny, Johnny – what's happening?"

"Here, Elmer, take these! Don't worry, we'll get out of here." John stood up and handed Elmer the black rosary beads that Padre LeFleur had given him at Lasang. John knew that the young man wasn't Catholic, but it was the only thing he had that he could give him. As Elmer took the rosary beads, a second torpedo slammed into the ship, cutting through the walls of the front hold. There was a terrific explosion, followed by hissing noises and a trembling sensation. John blacked out for a few seconds as seawater rushed in and it became very dark in the hold. He was holding his breath and could feel himself being violently tossed from side to side, tumbling in the water.

He opened his eyes in the water. Everything was dark, almost pitch black. Then he began to see some light, and he headed for it. As he was swimming, the color of the water was getting lighter and lighter. He didn't know how much longer he could hold his breath, and he was afraid he wasn't going to make it. Just as he was about to give up and open his mouth, he popped up on the surface of the ocean about 500 feet away from the ship.

Other POWs on the ship had similar experiences. Lieutenant Morris Shoss was knocked unconscious by the first torpedo. When he came to, everything was very quiet for he had been partially deafened by the explosions. There were dead bodies all around, and steel beams and decking had collapsed into the hold. He saw a rope dangling down from a gaping hole in the deck. He stumbled over dead bodies and somehow managed to pull himself up and slide onto the deck. The bodies of dead Japanese guards were all over the deck. Lieutenant Shoss jumped overboard just in time to escape one guard who was aiming his rifle at him.

After the first torpedo hit and the guards began firing machine guns and tossing grenades into the holds, one of the grenades landed next to the left foot of Marine PFC Verle Cutter. He kicked it under some boards and it went off, putting nine fragments into his left leg, four into his right leg and three into each arm. As he was climbing up the steel ladder to the deck, a big rush of seawater came up from the hold and washed him right out onto the deck. It saved his life, but many of the POWs below him didn't make it out of the hold.

As Marine Corporal Onnie Clem, Jr. was swimming away, he noticed that there were little spurts of water hitting all around him; the Japanese guards were shooting at him. He could see another POW up ahead of him hanging onto a plank. The spurts of water quickly headed in his direction. Suddenly, the other POW stiffened and sank below the surface. He saw four or five other American POWs treading water nearby, so Corporal Clem headed towards them. Then, the little spurts of water headed towards the other group and, one by one, they all disappeared below the surface.

Private Harry Meson's luck ran out that afternoon. As the ship was sinking, he was standing by a hatch throwing boards over the side for other POW's to use as life preservers. Suddenly, a bullet from a guard's rifle slammed into him, and the board he was holding flew into the air. After being hit, he spun around twice and fell into the water.

Lieutenant John Playter managed to make it to what was left of the deck, and he dived overboard just as the ship started to sink. He was pulled down into the water by the suction of the sinking ship. As he was going down, he was struck by something that ripped his left leg, left arm, left wrist and shoulder. Somehow, he managed to turn himself around and headed for the surface. The first person he saw was Lieutenant Gene Dale, who said, "We're free men. Let's get the hell out of here."

The two had not swum very far when they came across Jim Light, a Navy PT man. Jim had been shot in the right shoulder after he escaped from the ship. The bullet had entered through his back and exited from the small of his right shoulder, leaving a gaping hole. He was stubbornly holding onto a piece of wreckage with his feet and his left arm, but he was losing the battle. Every time his shoulder came out of the water, blood spurted uncontrollably. The two men worked with Light for about 30 minutes before Light finally said, "Boys, I'm not gonna make it, and if you guys keep trying to help me, you won't either. Thanks for trying." A short time later, he died and slowly sank into the sea. John Playtor and Gene Dale were later joined by Bert Schwartz and Verle Cutter, and the four began making their way towards shore.

Two other POWs, Michael Pulce and Victor Mapes, had also managed to escape the sinking ship. They met under a hatch cover that was floating on the surface and had about a foot of airspace under it. When a Japanese guard who was also in the water tried to stab them with his bayonet, they drowned him. They took his canteen and drank the contents.

Peter Golino and Chuck Claybourn had managed to make it to the deck of the Shinyo Maru. Pete looked down at the water and told Chuck, "There's no way I'm jumping down there."

"Oh yes you are. Just do what I tell you." Chuck said, as he pulled Pete over the side with him. They found a ladder floating nearby, and Chuck told Pete to hang onto the back of it and kick his legs. Every once in a while, a Japanese plane would come over and strafe the men in the water, causing them to duck under the waves. On one of these strafing runs, Pete got shot in the knee.

John Mackowski didn't know how he had gotten out of the ship. He figured he had been blown out. The current was very strong, and he was being swept away from the ship. At first, he thought he was alone. Directly in front of him, but quite a distance away, he could see the green hills of Mindanao Island.

Behind him was a scene that Hollywood could not reproduce. The bow of the Shinyo Maru was a lot lower in the water than the stern, which had a gaping hole in it. The stern was all crumpled, and he could see the propellers sticking out of the water. Steam and smoke were coming out of the ship and its foghorn was blowing. Japanese soldiers and sailors were running around on the deck. The sea, as far as John could see in every direction, was littered with the bodies, and parts of bodies, of dead American POWs.

Then, about 100 yards away, John saw Lieutenant Hashimoto standing on some sort of a float holding a Japanese flag attached to a small pole. He was trying to lead a few Japanese soldiers in singing their national anthem. There was a point when John's and Hashimoto's eyes met. They looked directly at each other for a few seconds. Then, John, with half a smile on his face, put his thumb to his nose and gave the lieutenant the "five finger salute." He didn't know why he did it, but it felt good. Almost immediately, the lieutenant fired two shots at John, one splashing into the water about two feet to the left of him and the other about the same distance to the right. John ducked under the water. By the time he surfaced, the current had carried the lieutenant and his raft further away. The Shinyo Maru slowly slipped below the surface with only the single smokestack still showing.

Army Captain William Cain had managed to get to the deck of the ship by climbing up one of the steel beams that had partially fallen into the hold. He quickly made his way to the stern of the ship and jumped off as the guards began shooting at him. He managed to partially camouflage himself in the water after finding a blue shirt and a piece of a grass mat floating nearby. He positioned them carefully on his head so he could breathe and still see where he was going. Japanese seaplanes were flying low over the water shooting at the Americans as they tried to escape.

As Captain Cain was slowly swimming away from the sinking ship, he too, saw Lieutenant Hashimoto on a raft with several Japanese soldiers. He watched in horror as the guards paddled the raft towards POWs in the water. Each time the raft got close to an American, Lieutenant Hashimoto would take his sword and hack away at their heads.

John was suffering from severe pain in his right side and was having trouble swimming because of it. He could not move his right hand or lift his right arm because of the pain, so he started to dog-paddle towards the island. As he headed towards the shore, he was getting weaker and didn't think he was going to make it. Then he saw four other POWs hanging onto a large wooden ladder just a few yards away. He called over, "Hey, you guys got room for one more?"

"Yeah, there's always room for one more."

John recognized the voice right away. It was Chuck Claybourn, a Navy man in his early 20's.

"Thanks," John said as he began to swim towards them. As he headed over in their direction, however, the pain was becoming unbearable and was sapping his strength.

"I don't think I'm gonna make it guys, but thanks anyway," John told them.

"Listen Polack, if you took that guardhouse rap, you can take this. Now get your sorry ass over here," Claybourn yelled back.

The words of the Navy man seemed to spur John on, and he somehow managed to get up the strength to dog-paddle his way to them. When he reached them, he was so exhausted he had all he could do just to hang on.

"Don't worry, John, we'll get you in," Claybourn said.

John thought to himself that it was an ironic coincidence that it was a Navy man who caused him to spend 22 days in the guardhouse, and now it was a Navy man who was helping him out in his time of need. There was no doubt that Chuck Claybourn's words saved John's life that day.

Just as the five exhausted men reached a coral reef, the Japanese ran a large empty tanker straight onto the beach. The men guessed they did this so the American submarine could not hit it broadside and sink it. John, Chuck Claybourn, Peter Golino and two other

POWs did not dare to come ashore during daylight because there was a Japanese machine gunner positioned midship on the beached tanker with the machine gun aimed in their direction. The machine gunner was firing at any POW he saw alive in the water or wading onto the beach. The five decided to hide behind the coral reef until nightfall.

There was a full moon that night, and it was very bright when they finally decided to take their chances and swim to shore. When they landed on the beach, they quickly headed into the jungle where they met a couple of other POWs — Captain Robert Blakeslee, Staff Sergeant Hayes Bolitho and Private Marco Caputo. When John saw Caputo, they shook hands and Caputo said:

"There's not many of us who made it, John."

"Yeah, I know," John replied.

"Gee! I hope we get out of here." Caputo said.

"Don't worry. We'll make it," John replied.

At that point, Captain Blakeslee made the decision that he would be the point man for the group. If, by chance, they encountered any Japanese soldiers, they were all to take off in different directions. Seeing that John was in severe pain, one of the other POWs tied his web belt around John's chest to keep any broken ribs from sticking him and causing any further injury.

About a mile into the jungle, two Filipinos jumped in front of the group, scaring the hell out of them. Then, they motioned with their hands for the Americans to follow them. The Filipinos took the group to a small barrio where they met 19 other POW survivors. Many of them were injured and they were in shock that they were now free. They couldn't fully comprehend what had happened, and they didn't really know what to do. Most of them were still afraid to make a move without someone telling them to. If one of the Filipinos told them to go to a particular place or in a certain direction, the POW's went there without question.

John had no clothes. He was completely nude except for the string from the Japanese underwear he had been wearing. He had to walk amongst the natives that way. Every time a man, woman, or even a child looked at him, it made him very uncomfortable.

The Filipinos gave the Americans water and made them a dinner of cracked corn and fish heads. John kept chewing a fish head until it finally went down. While he was eating his dinner, a Filipino woman made some gestures to John asking what was wrong. He indicated that he thought something was broken. She began crying and left. Shortly thereafter, he felt a hand gently rubbing his back. The woman was rubbing his back with a greasy substance, and it felt pretty good. John didn't do or say anything because he saw several Filipino men standing around, and they all had bolo knives. After dinner, John was unable to lie down, so he spent the night sitting on a bench.

That first night in the guerrilla camp, one of the survivors died. In the prison camps, he had always moaned that he did not feel well, and rarely went out on work details. His fellow POWs gave him the nickname "goldbrick." When he landed on the beach after escaping from the ship, he claimed he did not feel well and had pains in his chest. Another POW, who knew him, told him, "Cut out the horse shit. We're all hurting and no one else is complaining." The next day, he was dead from a bad case of pneumonia. One of the guys said that he had "cried wolf once too often" and when he was really sick, no one believed him.

The next morning, September 8th, the ranking POW officer, Lt. Colonel Harry Fischer, made the decision to move the group further inland. He was afraid the Japanese would be coming after them. Some POWs rode in water-buffalo-drawn carts, but there was not enough room for John, even though he had broken ribs and was in excruciating pain. Along the way, they ran into other POW survivors who had been found by the Filipinos near the beach. One of them was Jack Donohue, who had been in the water for over 24 hours and had severe sunburn. The group of POW survivors, whose numbers increased along the way ever so slightly, climbed up and down the hills heading towards the guerrilla base camp.

As they were very near the camp, John sat down on a rock and looked out at the ocean. It was at that point that he realized that the war would soon be over for him. He thought, I'm going home. I can't believe it, but I'm actually going home. As he was thinking this, a fellow POW survivor, Jim McComas from the 192nd Tank Battalion stopped by. When Jim McComas was swimming away from the sinking ship, he saw a Japanese guard in the water who had a big smile on his face. McComas swam up behind the guard, held his head under the water and drowned him.

"Hey, John, do you need any help walking?" McComas asked.

"No, thanks. I'll be alright as soon as I catch my breath," John replied.

"You sure? I'll help you," McComas said.

"Thanks. I'm alright," John said.

He was the last POW to make it to the camp that night.

John also felt a great deal of pain in his ears, and noticed that puss was coming out of them. A Filipino woman gave him a bandana off of her head to wrap around his head because the flies and other bugs were buzzing around his ears. A Filipino doctor, Doctor Calo, put some yellow-colored anti-gangrene medicine in John's ears, and it cleared up.

Sometime later, as the entire group moved further inland, John got a bad case of diarrhea. He had it so bad, he joked, that he thought he was leaving a trail for the Japanese to follow (but they never did). Moro tribesmen built a thatched lean-to for the men. It was covered with nipa grass on three sides, and thatched with nipa for the roof. An elderly Filipino woman worked on John's broken ribs and somehow managed to set them.

On the second morning, Colonel Fisher ordered the men to fall in. He told them that Colonel John McGee had joined the group during the night and would be the new commanding officer. Colonel McGee had been stationed in this part of the Philippines before the war. He was one of two officers who jumped off different Japanese ships and swam to shore. The second officer, Lieutenant Wills from the 26th Cavalry, was the man whom John was going to escape with back at Davao. Colonel McGee would be going out with the men, and Lieutenant Wills would be staying behind with the guerrillas. Private Coe, a survivor who was a radio operator, would also be staying behind with the guerrillas. The men were eating pretty well and starting to get stronger, but John still did not have any pants.

"For God's sake, get me a pair of pants!" John pleaded with the Filipinos, and he eventually received a pair of shorts to cover his lower body. They were quite worn in the rear and had a big tear, but John didn't mind because at least they covered his front.

He was also given a carbine and some ammunition. The date stamp on the carbine was 1-11-44, less than a year old. He asked one of the Filipino guerrillas, Sergeant Caliso, how they managed to get it. His answer was "The submarine Sir." John just smiled. Now he knew that, finally, help would be on the way – a little bit late, but it would be welcomed all the same, even after such a long delay.

The Americans remained with the guerrillas for about a month. Rumor had it that a submarine would be taking them out. They didn't know how many of them the submarine could take out, so each of the men was given a number, based on how badly he was hurt. John got number twelve. He thought, I must be in pretty rough shape. There's eighty-two of us going out, and I've got number twelve.

The group had gone down to the beach once, but the submarine didn't show. Then, very late one other night, almost two o'clock in the morning, they saw the signal: a bonfire many miles away. They slowly made their way down the steep jungle hillside to the beach. It was a dark, moonless night.

The men jumped into small boats with outriggers, called "boncas," manned by Filipinos. Each of these boats could take only one, two or three men. John was in a small boat with another POW survivor, and there were two Filipinos paddling. About fifteen minutes later, they came alongside a huge black thing in the water. It was a submarine, the USS Narwhal, a large submarine that the Navy used mostly for supplying the guerrillas and taking people in and out of hot spots. A big Navy man extended his hand to John and pulled him up on deck. John practically flew out of the bonca. The sailor smiled and said, "Step lively."

"Move fast. Just follow the line and keep moving," another sailor said.

John could see a small red light coming from inside of the submarine. He headed towards the rear of the submarine deck and climbed through the hatch and down the ladder. It was at this point that the men finally realized that they were back under the control of an American officer on an American ship. They knew they were finally safe and on their way home. It was a tremendous feeling of relief and pride that no one who had not experienced what they had experienced could ever know.

As John sat on the floor with his fellow POW survivors, the USS Narwhal got underway and slowly slipped below the surface. John thought how great it was to be an American. He felt like hugging every sailor on the ship who had come to take him home. But his feelings of joy were mixed with some uncertainty. He was surprised to see such large numbers of healthy servicemen, the clean conditions under which they were living and the modern military equipment they were using. Just hearing the American language over the loudspeakers was a pleasure, as was hearing the nickname "Ski," used to describe an American with a long Polish name. For John, the battle with the Japanese was over, but the battle to return to civilian life was just beginning.

Chapter 11

THE TRIP HOME
October 1944

The former POW's first meal on the submarine was a ham sandwich and a cup of tomato soup. It was John's first American meal in quite a long time, and it tasted real good. For the next six days aboard the submarine, the group ate like there was no tomorrow. The submarine's cook had a lot of trouble keeping them all fed. As they crossed the Equator, the men received the "King Neptune Rites," (A traditional initiation given to all new submariners.) although the Navy men went easy on the group of survivors. Without hesitation, John was the first Army "draftee" to receive the "King Neptune Rites" aboard the USS Narwhal.

Six days later, the submarine arrived at a Navy base called Windy Island, located somewhere in the northern part of New Guinea. As the survivors came up on the deck of the USS Narwhal, the crewmembers were standing in formation. As each of the survivors passed by, the crewmembers gave them a salute. When John saw this wonderful show of support, tears welled up in his eyes, but they did not flow.

The Navy personnel on shore gave the group the biggest breakfast they could imagine. It was the first time that many of these men had ever sat at a table with white linen on it and it had been a long time since any of them sat at any table. Some of the guys ate so much that they got sick.

The next day, the men received plain khaki uniforms with no markings on them. After cursory medical examinations were completed, the group was put into a Higgins boat and taken to Pie Island, an Air Corps base. It was the first time John and the other survivors saw the new helmets troops were now wearing, and the first time they had seen a Higgins boat, which was a smaller version of an LST (Landing Ship Tanks, although the Navy men liked to call them "Large Slow Targets!")

As the boat approached the shore, the ramp on the front began to open up. As it was lowered, the men could see about a hundred American military people standing on each side, including nurses and doctors. As John walked down the ramp, he could smell the nurses' perfume, but for some reason he couldn't look at them. The fact that they were looking at him made him feel very uncomfortable.

A doctor with the last name of Wilson, who came from Chicago, treated John's ear. Military personnel asked the former POW's all sorts of questions. John and a fellow POW survivor named Bill Haskell, a staff sergeant who hailed from Rhode Island, went before a group of soldiers to answer some questions.

"How can you guys smile after all you have been through?" one soldier asked John.

"After you see and smell death all the time, what else can happen to you!" John said.

They wanted to know all sorts of things about the Japanese, and asked if they had seen particular Americans alive in the prison camps, etc. All of the POW survivors had been instructed by an Army intelligence officer that there were certain things the government didn't want them to talk about. If the questions got too sticky, they were just to tell the person asking the questions that they couldn't answer because they were "Project J" men.

The next morning after breakfast, a group of 20 to 25 survivors flew out of Pie Island on a DC-47, a green Army twin-engine plane with a big star on it. The men sat along the walls on two seats that ran the length of the plane on either side. It was John's first airplane ride ever. After about an hour into their flight, as they were flying over some islands off the coast of New Guinea, the flight sergeant came over and told the group, "There's over 20,000 Japs down there."

"Then keep this bucket going! I've had enough of those bastards!" John yelled out.

Later in the flight, the sergeant came around with a clipboard asking the survivors to sign their names on a sheet of paper, which he called his "short snorter." All of them signed, except John. After the flight sergeant had collected all of the names except for John's, he came back to John and again asked him to sign his name on the paper.

"Why won't you sign your name on the paper? the sergeant asked. "You don't want my name on that paper. You want somebody that's important," John said.

"You guys are important. Everyone else signed the paper, why not you?" the sergeant replied as he handed John the clipboard. John took the clipboard and looked down the list of names. When he saw the name "Colonel Charles A. Lindbergh" he asked for the sergeant's pen and signed it right under Lindbergh's name.

"What made you finally sign your name?" the sergeant asked. "When I saw Colonel Charles Lindbergh's name on the sheet, I decided to sign my name," John replied.

"Why is that?" the sergeant asked.

"Lindbergh was the only one who spoke up before World War II and told the American people that the Germans had the best air force in the world. For his honesty, he was called a Nazi lover, but to me, he was a true American," John said.

The sergeant told John a few stories about Lindbergh, including one about how he trained P-38 fighter pilots in New Guinea. Sometimes, Lindbergh would take off with a P-38 and come back with his ammo well spent. He eventually got called back to the States because he was only a civilian at the time and wasn't supposed to be shooting at the enemy. [Note: It was a good thing that John signed that paper. The sergeant and his "short snorter" eventually wound up in Manchuria picking up some other American survivors, including a member of John's old company, Felix Kozakevitch. When Felix saw John's name on the list, he asked the flight sergeant about it, and that's how he knew that John had also made it home.]

The group stayed overnight at a small military base in New Guinea. Before they took off the next morning, a group of newspaper photographers showed up and began taking pictures of them. John wandered off and stood underneath the wing of the plane, looking at the destruction on the runway, including the skeletal remains of many burned up planes near the runway. He also noticed that there was a house on a nearby hill that apparently had not been touched by any Japanese bombing. Just then, two generals drove up to John in a jeep. One was a two-star general and the other was a one-star general. As they stopped next to him, John saluted and the generals returned the salute.

"Hey, soldier! How was it up north?" one of them asked.

"I don't know what you're talking about, Sir," John replied, thinking that this might be some sort of a test. After all, he had been told not to talk too much about what had happened to him.

"Why aren't you over there with the other POW's having your picture taken?" the second general asked.

"I guess I just don't go in for that kind of stuff," John replied. Then he asked, "Tell me: how come that house wasn't hit?"

The generals both smiled. Then one said, "Did you know that General MacArthur stayed at that house?"

John didn't answer. He thought they were trying to prod him into saying something that he'd be sorry for, so he waited for the next question.

"Did you know he also had a bathtub flown in on a military plane for his personal use?"

"I guess some people like to live in comfort no matter where they are," John answered, somewhat sarcastically.

The generals both smiled, and one of them said, "Welcome home, son. We knew where you were." Then they shook his hand. John saluted and they drove away in their jeep.

The group then got back on the plane and headed for their next stop, Australia. During the flight, they saw a large flotilla of American ships heading north. Before dark, the plane landed in Thompsonville, Australia, where they boarded a bus driven by a female Australian Army corporal. She really knew how to drive that bus, especially at night. She was driving without lights under blackout conditions. One of the survivors, Marco Caputo, tried to hit on her, and she put him in his place rather quickly.

A short time later, the bus arrived at the 42nd General Hospital in Brisbane. The officers and enlisted men were separated. For the next two weeks, the men stayed at the hospital to recuperate, and they were allowed to eat as much as they could. John gained thirteen pounds during this short hospital stay. One day, Mrs. Douglas MacArthur came in to visit the men in the ward, escorted by two "full bird" colonels. When she came in, all of them stood by their beds, almost as if they were under inspection. She walked slowly down the ward talking with each and every man.

"What outfit were you with?" she asked John.

"I was a member of Company A, 803rd Aviation Engineers," John answered.

"I know you boys. You used to go back and forth on Corregidor," She said.

"Yes, Ma'am, I was one of them." The two colonels broke out in broad smiles.

"I'm glad you made it out of there. Have a safe trip home," she said as she shook John's hand.

"Thank you for stopping by to see us," John said. Then, as quickly as she had come, she left.

While at the 42nd General Hospital, John saw his first movie in two and a half years. It was "White Christmas" starring Bing Crosby and Barry Fitzgerald, and it did make John's eyes a bit misty. Then, the orders came that the group would be going back to the States. The night before they left, the doctors and nurses threw a big party with food, music, beer and booze. The guys were dancing with the nurses and having a great time. Most got very drunk. One of the nurses, Lieutenant Una Louise Black, who everyone called "Blackie," gave John a bottle of scotch just before he left.

The next morning, they boarded the USS Monterey, a large transport that had been a cruise ship before the war, and headed east. There were no escort ships because the Monterey could go 24 knots, faster than any enemy submarine. They had some lifeboat drills, but John never participated. He just stayed in his cabin. One day, John's Navy friend, Chuck Claybourn, asked him, "What the hell are you going to do if we're torpedoed and your still in your cabin?"

"Chuck, I really don't give a shit," John replied.
Halfway to the States, John pulled out the bottle of scotch given to him by "Blackie" and opened it. He was offered twenty-five bucks for it, but he shared it with his buddies instead.

Rumor had it that the ship was taking a longer route because a Japanese submarine had sunk an American transport somewhere along the original route. The ship finally arrived in San Francisco on November 7, 1944, and as it passed under the Golden Gate Bridge, the men were cheering.

The group stayed at Fort McDowell for about ten days. John wrote his second V-mail letter to Opal shortly after he arrived at McDowell. During his stay there, John had two incidents that affected him. He was in the mess hall having breakfast, and seated at the same table were two Army sergeants and a fellow wearing a windbreaker with a patch depicting Italy on his sleeve. It was a green patch with white lettering. Nothing was said until after the guy with the patch left. Then, John turned to the two sergeants and asked, "Tell me, was that guy in the Italian campaign?" They both looked at John like he was some kind of a nut. Then one Sergeant said, "I don't know where you've been, but that guy is an Italian prisoner of war."

John was so angry he couldn't talk. He was upset because of how nice the Americans were treating the enemy POW's. He slammed his fork down on the plate, got up and walked away from the table. John didn't tell the two sergeants who he was or what he had been through.

On another occasion, John and Marco Caputo decided to take a walk around the island. It was a chilly day, a good day for a walk. As they were walking along, they came upon a fenced enclosure with barbed wire on top. Within the enclosure, they saw Japanese POWs talking and laughing, wearing nice clean warm uniforms. For a moment, the two survivors were petrified at the sight of Japanese soldiers. When they overcame the shock, they started to curse them, calling them all sorts of names in Japanese. Caputo, in particular, could speak pretty good Japanese. The Japanese POW's all became quiet and just looked at John and Marco.

All of a sudden, a military policeman came along and said, "Hey, you two! Cut it out!" The MP didn't know what they were saying to the Japanese, but he got the drift of it. "Move along before you get into trouble," the MP told them, and they left.

Finally, John and Marco Caputo were given orders to go by train to Fort Dix, New Jersey. John wrote to Opaline and told her he was coming home. Before they left the train station in San Francisco, a young lady came up to them and asked if they knew her brother, who was in the Marine Corps. She showed them a picture of him, and John thought he recognized him from one of the POW camps. She asked John if her brother was on the ship that was torpedoed and John said that, to the best of his knowledge, he wasn't on that ship.

Then, they heard the conductor yell "all aboard," and they jumped on the train. It was a really slow-moving train, but that didn't matter — they were going home. The train stopped in Pueblo, Colorado, for about three hours. The conductor told John and Marco to go take a walk. Instead, they decided to grab a cab and head into town. They went to a bar and had a few beers, then John brought a bottle of booze in a liquor store. Marco, who thought he was God's gift to women, was trying to pick up a local girl when they heard the train whistle blowing.

"Oh shit! The train's leaving," Marco said.

"So what? We'll catch the next one," John replied.

"The hell we will! My money's on that train. Let's get the hell out of here!" Marco yelled. They took off running as fast as they could, with John laughing all the way back. Luckily, the conductor saw them coming and held the train until they got on board.

The next day, John and Marco invited the conductor to have a drink with them. He was really a nice guy. He told them that his son was in the service somewhere in the Pacific. John thought the conductor knew who they were, but he never asked them any questions. John thought that was probably the reason he held the train for them.

The rest of the train ride was uneventful. After a brief stop in Chicago, they went on to Fort Dix.

When they arrived at Fort Dix, they walked over to the desk sergeant. Now, Marco had the orders for both he and John. They had been printed on one sheet of paper. Marco held onto them because his last name began with the letter "C" and, at that time, the Army did a lot of things alphabetically. The sergeant, who had a nasty disposition, asked Marco, "Where are the furlough papers for both of you."

"This is the only paperwork they gave us," Marco told the sergeant.

"How come you don't have your own orders?" the sergeant asked John. By this time, John had had just about enough.

"Hey, Sarge, why don't you go take a shit for yourself and leave us alone."

"Do you know who you're talking to?" the sergeant angrily asked.

"Yeah, just another asshole," John replied.

"John, please stay out of it," Marco pleaded, knowing John had a short fuse when it came to incompetent bureaucratic jerks. The sergeant made a move like he was going to come around the desk and of course, John was still yelling at him. Just then, a lieutenant came out of his office and asked the sergeant what was going on. The sergeant told him what happened, and that John was giving him a hard time. The lieutenant turned to John and said, "What outfit are you guys with, and where did you come from?"

"Sir, all I have to say to you is that I'm a "Project J" man," John said.

The lieutenant smiled and said, "We were told you people were coming. Come with me to the Major's office."

So Marco and John went to see the major, who gave them a "canned" spiel. He welcomed them home, schmoozed a little with them and then said, "I'm going to give both of you a twenty-one day leave."

"Wait a minute, Major. I've never had a furlough since I've been in the Army. According to the rules, I'm entitled to thirty days a year," John said.

"I'm only authorized to give you twenty-one days," the major responded.

"Then get your MP's ready, 'cause I'm not coming back in twenty-one days," John said. He and Marco took their passes, left the office and headed to their homes.

Some of Marco's relatives came to Fort Dix to take him home and they gave John a lift into lower Manhattan, to Canal Street. From there, John took the subway uptown to 42nd Street and then transferred to the IND train to Brooklyn. He didn't know whether to go home first, or to Opaline's house. He didn't want to give his parents a shock, so he decided to go to Opaline's house first. He walked up to her apartment and knocked on the door. Opaline opened the door, and when she saw John, she gave him a big hug and a lot of kisses.

"How come you didn't come in on the train from New Jersey? Me and Irene [Opaline's sister] went to Grand Central Station a couple of times to meet you."

"I got a lift to Manhattan from Marco's relatives."

After a short visit there, John and Opaline headed out to John's parents' apartment house. They decided that Opaline should go in first to break the news to his mother and father. Opaline knocked on the door.

"Who's there?" John's mother yelled through the door.

"It's me, Opaline."

"Come in."

"Mom, I want you to stay calm, but I have a surprise for you out in the hallway."

"What kind of a surprise?" John's mother asked.

"John's out in the hall."

When John heard this, he walked in. His mother smiled at first, but then she started to cry tears of joy. After the excitement died down, John asked about the rest of the family. Soon, family members started to arrive at his mother's apartment, and John was thankful that none of them asked about his ordeal at the hands of his Japanese captors.

About a week after John arrived home, Lieutenant D'Amico from Fort Hamilton stopped by the apartment to visit him. The lieutenant told John that he could have an honorable discharge now, but he was advising against it because John might be eligible for some benefits if he hung in a little longer. Opaline told John now that he was stateside, she thought he should be patient and stay in the Army a little longer. John went along with them. Two days later, Lieutenant Leo O'Brien telephoned Opaline at her parent's apartment (John's parents didn't have a telephone) to tell her that John's leave was extended to ninety days.

At this point, Opal and John decided to get married. They set the date: February 4, 1945. The next weeks were filled with making arrangements for the wedding — selecting the band, the hall, inviting the guests and so forth. John's brother Chester would be his best man, and Opal's sister Irene would be her maid of honor.

As a result of his POW experience, John had developed a fear of crowds. He tried to use side streets when he walked Opal home now. He didn't understand it himself, but he felt he could only trust his family and, of course Opal. She was not only the girl he was going to marry, but also his best friend.

John and Captain Bert Schwartz were the guests of New York City Mayor Fiorello LaGuardia one Sunday on his radio show. The two POW survivors sat in front of a huge microphone and answered questions from the mayor and members of the audience. One of the questions was a little strange.

"Corporal, did you ever call a Jap a monkey?" the mayor asked John.

"I've called them a lot of things, but I never called them that," John replied.

The Mayor had a great big smile on his face and the fifty or so people in the audience laughed. After the show, some people came up to John and Bert and asked for their autographs.

On February 4, 1945, John and Opaline were married at St. Cecelia and St. Methodias Church. They had their reception at the Grand Street Ballroom. After the reception, John and Opal stayed for a week at the St. George Hotel, in downtown Brooklyn. They stayed there because a week later John was scheduled for a two-week R&R (rest and relaxation) leave in Florida, and Opal, as John's wife, would go with him as the guest of the government. On February 11, 1945, they boarded a train at Penn Station and headed to Florida. They had a compartment all to themselves. Their first hotel in Florida was the Alden Hotel in Miami Beach, which served a buffet-style breakfast each morning. Every once in a while, John had to go off to be debriefed, but the rest of the time they were left to enjoy themselves. They went swimming, fishing, dancing and sightseeing, and they began to look ahead to their new life together.

EPILOG

Their son Gregory was born in 1945. John, Opal, Gregory, and Opal's mother and father left Greenpoint in December of 1950 and moved upstate to Austerlitz, in Columbia County. A few years later, their daughter Marlene was born. John worked for Columbia Box Company in Chatham for awhile, and then for General Electric in Pittsfield, Massachusetts. While he was at GE, he was elected president of local 255 of the International Union of Electrical Workers. He was very active in the Austerlitz Volunteer Fire Department, eventually becoming chief.

John was one of a handful of ex-POW's who fought to get special license plates for those who had been prisoners of war. John picked "POW-83" in honor of the 83 men who survived the sinking of the Shinyo Maru and made it to shore on September 7, 1944.

Today's Americans owe a debt of gratitude to all of the men and women who fought in our wars to preserve the precious freedoms that many of us take for granted. Too many of them made the ultimate sacrifice, and millions of others have been physically disfigured and/or psychologically scarred by their experiences.

John Mackowski, like many millions of others, was just another guy from a lower-middle-class family who got drafted into the service to fight a war. I believe that what he went through at the hands of his ruthless captors had to be written down so that it will never be forgotten. I wrote John's story, not so much for himself, but for his family and especially his grandchildren, so that they might know that their grandfather tried to do what was right, and in doing so, underwent severe punishment.

So, the next time you see a person drive by with a prisoner of war plate on his or her car, take a good look at them. And when you are sitting on a bus or a train, or passing through an airport, take a good look at some of the older people you see there. Because I'll guarantee that some of them, just like John Mackowski, have also been to hell and back.

APPENDIX

The following pages contain the statements of fellow soldiers who were prisoners of war with John Mackowski. These brave men witnessed John Mackowski in the POW camps, and they have attested to some of the abusive treatment that John received at the hands of his captors. These statements have been transcribed and typed in order that they fit the format of the book.

Also included here are the names of the eighty-three (83) survivors of the Shinyo Maru, some pictures of John Mackowski and his wife Opal, and even three of his favorite "POW" recipes.

STATEMENTS OF FELLOW
PRISONERS OF WAR

GILBERT B. SOIFER

JOHN J. MORETT

JOHN R. BENNETT

CHARLES V. CLAYBOURN

WILLIAM P. CAIN

STATEMENT OF GILBERT B. SOIFER

My name is Gilbert B. Soifer. I live at 7345 Malverne Avenue, Philadelphia, Pa. 19151. I was a member of Company A, 803rd Engineer Battalion, Aviation, Separate. I held the rank of Sergeant. My Army Serial Number was 33028005.

In January of 1942, my unit, (Company A, 803rd) was stationed on the West Coast of the Bataan Peninsula on the Island of Luzon in the Philippines.

On January 24, 1942, my unit (Company A, 803rd) was ordered to proceed to Agloma point. Elements of the 45th Infantry (Philippine Scouts) were among the various units engaged in combat at Agloma Point.

In April of 1942, my unit (Company A, 803rd) was ordered to proceed to Monkey Point on Corregidor. Elements of the 31st Infantry (USA) were among the units engaged in combat at Monkey Point.

Company A, 803rd Engineer Battalion, suffered many casualties in both of these engagements. In fact, I was wounded at Agloma Point (gunshot wound to the chest) and then at Monkey Point (shell fragmentation wound to upper thigh).

John Mackowski, (Army Serial Number 32109397) of Austerlitz, New York, was a member of Company A, 803rd Engineer Battalion. He was present with me at both Agloma Point on Bataan and Monkey Point on Corregidor, Philippine Islands.

To all the above I swear to.

Signed: Gilbert B. Soifer
Sworn to and subscribed before me, a Notary Public, in Narberth, Pennsylvania (Montgomery County). Richard A. Blankley, 4/2/83.

STATEMENT OF JOHN J. MORETT

May 3, 1973

To Whom It May Concern:

This is to state that I know John Mackowski and that he was a prisoner of war with me at the Lasang Work Camp under the control of the Japanese from March through August 1944. John was incarcerated in a cell for 22 days when he was involved in the stealing of some wire shears while on a kitchen detail with nine other men. A prisoner named _____ [the name is purposely not included in this book] had put the sheers in a ration basket which John was carrying with another man. When it was discovered the shears were stolen, the detail was questioned. For the group, John confessed when the guilty person remained silent, thus saving the whole detail from punishment.

Without delay, John was placed in a cell, stripped of all clothing and made to stand at attention and not allowed to sleep except when he would fall unconscious to the floor. They would prod him awake and force John to stand again. There were times when he was forced to kneel, but with his back in an upright position. This put pressure on his legs causing loss of circulation and induced swelling and pain. He received one-third cup of water a day and a small amount of rice, which was sometimes dumped out by the guards. The American medical officer, aware of the small ration, ground up some vitamin pills, mixing the powder with the rice to give John some added strength. There was a confrontation at one point between John and Lieutenant Hashimoto. Due to this, he was tied up, arms outward, knees half bent but off the floor, so that he was placed in a most uncomfortable position. Then he was beaten with a rod. Eventually he passed out. He related later to a number of us that when he became conscious, he was bleeding from the mouth and nose, his legs were badly swollen and he was unable to rise up from the floor.

During this period of time, some of the prisoners on their way to work would call out to John with words of encouragement. Prayer and tenacity helped bring him through this terrible ordeal. Upon his release one of the Japanese officers said to him: "You paid the penalty and we admire you as a soldier. We know you shielded someone else."

I saw John when he returned to the American compound. He was thin, dehydrated, weak and bruised. All of us in the camp admired him for surviving the situation when his American manhood was severely tested.

These facts are true to the best of my knowledge and memory

John J. Morrett
Rector
St. Albans Church
Columbus, Ohio

Sworn to and subscribed in my presence this 7th Day of May, 1973 at Columbus, Ohio, Franklin County. By Raymond Hudson, Notary Public, Franklin County, Ohio.

LETTER OF JOHN R. BENNETT

To Whom it May Concern

Dear Sirs:

I have known John Mackowski of Austerlitz, N.Y., for many years, but the years that stand out in my mind the most are those years at Davao Penal Colony. We both were Prisoners of War of Japan until we were released by an accident of war. We were in a Japanese convoy going to Japan when we were sunk by an American submarine. There were 750 Americans aboard, and only 82 survived. [83 made it to shore, but This I inject into this letter as a matter of record of our association.

While at Davao Penal Colony, we were fed rice and greens which we named "King Kong." These greens grew in swamp, and we harvested it daily. The Japanese fed it to us along with rice. Our daily allowance was 800 grams of food a day. As you can see, soon we became sick with malnutrition, beri-beri, scurvy, malaria, pellegra and eye problems. We were forced to work, but you can imagine how much work we could perform.

Davao is situated in the middle of a jungle. It was always damp and wet. Our barracks consisted of sleeping on the floor, which further aggravated our condition. This is true. In fact it was brought out at the war trials, which took place in Tokyo and Manila after the war.

Yours truly,

John R. Bennett
Past National Commander of American Defenders
of Bataan and Corregidor.

Notarized by W. Eugenia Mazzara, Notary Public, State of
New York, September 12, 1978.

STATEMENT OF CHARLES V. CLAYBOURN

January 14, 1977

To Whom It May Concern:

This will attest that while a prisoner of war of the Japanese during the period May 1942 thru September 1944 at Military Prison Camp #2, Davao, Mindanao, Philippine Islands, Mr. John Mackowski, now residing in Austerlitz, N.Y., was held prisoner in the same camp. Consequently, I was in a position to observe Mr. Mackowski as regards his general health and physical condition during that period. He was badly emaciated and weak from the malnutrition and maltreatment. On at least one occasion he suffered from the onset of dysentery.

In August 1944, while on a work detail, Mr. Mackowski was removed from the main compound and placed in special custody in the Japanese guardhouse as punishment for an alleged violation of camp regulations. Having been singled out myself on three separate occasions for such punishment, I can attest to and sympathize with the vicious treatment of such confinement: beatings with bamboo, kicking, repeated slapping, starvation, denial of drinking water, hours of uninterrupted interrogation, denial of sleep or rest, uninterrupted hours of standing in the hot sun essentially naked, confinement in a small unventilated cell with a tin roof barely five feet above the floor, regular and sustained abusement by judo, binding in unnatural and painful positions, and general and unsupervised harassment by the Japanese guards. The guardhouse was only a few feet outside the main compound so while we could not see, we could plainly hear the interrogations with accompanied administration of punishments to Mr. Mackowski.

Mr. Mackowski was held twenty-two days in the guardhouse before being returned to the main compound. He was half-carried, half-dragged to the gate and thrown on the ground. After a short speech by a Japanese Officer (that the rules must be obeyed) he was released to the main compound. Carried to the barracks, he was cared for as well as possible without medical supplies. Specifically, there were three or four days during which it appeared doubtful that he would live; His arms, legs and face were badly swollen and after washing away the accumulated filth, we found his entire body was badly bruised and abraised.

Roughly one month later, in September 1944, Mr. Mackowski was one of only 83 men who survived the sinking of the Japanese prison ship Oryoko Maru (actually John was on the Shinyo Maru) off Mindanao Island in the Philippines. Still, in extra-ordinarily poor physical condition from his earlier punishment in the guardhouse, and having then spent nineteen days locked in the hold of the prison ship under conditions which were more than intolerable, then sustaining the shock and battering of torpedoing of the ship, it was bordering on the unthinkable that he was able to clear the sinking ship and attempt to swim to the island some three or four miles distance. I was in a position to observe Mr. Mackowski while in the water, since I was privileged to assist him in his effort. He appeared to have sustained some kind of chest injury since he was having difficulty breathing. It was my judgement that because of that difficulty, together with his questionable physical condition, due not only to his recent guardhouse experience, but also long and debilitating imprisonment, he likely would not have survived to reach the island, notwithstanding his personal will and determination.

Frankly, I am surprised indeed, that Mr. Mackowski has not suffered long before now serious and debilitating after-effects of his imprisonment and maltreatment at the hands of the Japanese.

It is not my purpose to dramatize or orate, but in retrospect I would suggest that there is no way the average one of us can adequately and understandably convey to another who has not himself experienced such imprisonment, the hopelessness, deprivation, loneliness, indiscriminate abusement and the unyielding day-after-day hunger and pain meted out by a divisive captor. In that context, I would plea with those who will evaluate the case of Mr. Mackowski, and in fact, any former POW, to h   e   e   d their utmost insight and compassion and to exercise not just the letter of the law, but further the spirit of the law.

Respectfully,

Charles V. Claybourn

Notarized by Carole M. Fox, on 1/18/77, Notary Public, Fairfield County, Ohio.

DEPOSITION OF CAPTAIN WILLIAM P. CAIN

Excerpts of deposition taken of Captain Cain, page 8, when questioned about the treatment of John Mackowski at the hands of the Japanese guards.

Captain. Do you recall the beating and mistreatment of Corporal John Mackowski during May of 1944?

Yes, I do. I did not see the actual beating, but it took place just outside the compound and almost in front of the barracks that he was living in, inside this house and I could hear Mackowski groaning. And I could hear apparently his body being thrown to the ground. I could hear his groans. I did not see it however.

Did you see Mackowski after this beating?

Not right after. After he was beaten he was placed in the guardhouse. I have forgotten the length of time that he was there, but I did see him after he was released from the guardhouse.

Were there any bruises or marks on his body after this beating?

After his release, I didn't notice any marks on his body but he looked like he had suffered a great deal and lost a lot of weight.

Commonwealth of the Philippines) SS
City of Manila)

Dated 6 March, 1946

I, Edwardo J. Manipula, residing at 661 Kundiman St., Sampaloc, Manila, P.I., being first duly sworn on oath, state that I truly and correct recorded and transcribed, the proceedings, and deposition of William P. Cain, Capt., Infantry.

THE NAMES OF THE 83 SURVIVORS
OF THE SHINYO MARU

Walter N. Alexander – Aurora, CO

John R. Bennett – Bethpage, NY

William E. Biddle – Toledo, OH

Jessie Bier – Lawrence, MA

Ray E. Billick – Vincennes, IN

Robert B. Blakeslee – Plattsburgh, NY

Hayes H. Bolitho – Big Sandy, TX

John W. Booth – Perham, MN

Paul L. Browning- Centralia, WA

William P. Cain – Camp McQuade, CA

Marco A. Caputo – Fort Edward, NY

William C. Chenoworth – San Antonio, TX

Charles V. Claburn – Beaufort, SC

Onnie E. Clem – Dallas, TX

D. J. Clinger – Denver, CO

Joseph P. Coe – Sierra Vista, AZ

Richard L. Cook – Los Angeles, CA

Verle D. Cutter – Needles, CA

Eugene R. Dale – March Field, CA

Harvey T. Denson – San Antonio, TX

Jack M. Donohue – Spokane, WA

James D. Donlon – Carmel, CA

Harry O. Fischer – Fort Belvoir, VA

William T. Frederick – Anaheim, CA

James A. Gardner – Glasgow, Scotland

Walter E. Gardner – Hopewell, VA

Frederick J. Gallagher – Oceanside, CA

Donald F. Gillen – Newport Beach, CA

John P. Gillespie – Iowa City, IA

Peter J. Golino – Irvine, CA

Donald J. Grantz – Fresno, CA

James R. Greene – Sawanee, GA

Issac B. Hagins – Phoenix, AZ

Willard E. Hall – Seattle, WA

Willard L. Haskell – Tucson, AZ

Francis Hoctor – Bidderford, ME

William S. Horabin – Austin, TX

Roy J. Hughes – Mountain Home, AR

Lawrence P. Ingley – Modesto, CA

Charles C. Johnstone – Washington, DC

Ralph R. Johnson – Sarasota, FL

Joseph H. Jones – Grove City, OH

Robert J. Kirker – Atlantic City, NJ

Lyle G. Knudson – Ogden, UT

Glen E. Kuskie – Florence. OR

Joseph C. Lamkin – Santa Barbara, CA

Calvin E. Latham – Rexburg, ID

Francis E. LeClear – Butler, PA

Bill J. Lorton – Medford, OR

John J. Mackowski – Ghent, NY

Victor L. Mapes – Silver Springs, MD

Cecil H. McClure – Dallas, TX

James F. McComas – Brainard, MN

John H. McGee – San Antonio, TX

Donald I. McPherson – Lincoln, NB

Lewis S. Moore – East Godsden, AL

John J. Morrett – Jacksonville, FL

Emery A. Motsinger – Ft. Leavenworth, KS

Cletus O. Overton – Little Rock, AK

Buster Parker – Clear Creek, WV

Ralph H. Person – Seattle, WA

Theodore L. Pflueger – Pacific Grove, CA

John C. Playter – Bolivar, MO

Michael Pulice – Las Cruces, NM

Otis E. Radcliff – Portsmouth, VA

George R. Robinette – Orangevale, CA

Denver R. Rose – Houston, TX

Roy D. Dussell – Forest Hill, CA

Omar A. Schoenborne – Cass Lake, MN

Bert Schwartz – Blairsville, GA

Felix C. Sharp Jr. – Ft. Benning, GA

Morris L. Shoss – San Antonio, TX

Marcus N. Simkins – Buda, IA

Harry J. Skinner – Berkeley, CA

Murray M. Sneddon – Burbank, CA

Paul S. Snowden – Glendale, CA

Charles A. Steinhauser – Oceanside, CA

John Stymelski – Detroit, MI

Lawrence Tipton – Capitola, CA

Edward S. Tresniewski – Cohoes, NY

James K. Vann – Winona, MO

Arthur D. Waters – Madera, CA

Harold W. Wilson – Nutwood, OH

Pictures of John Mackowski

John at the rifle range at Fort Belvoir, Virginia
in April of 1941

John

John on leave in Washington, DC
in June of 1941

John and Opal's Wedding on February 4, 1945

John and Opal in Miami in February 1945

John and Opal at Christmas 1993

JOHN'S "POW" RECIPES

During the course of their confinement in the various prison camps many American POWs became quite proficient in preparing tasty meals using what was available. John was no exception. Here are three of John's less than famous recipes:

Roasted Eggplant a la Davao

Several small eggplants - wash and slice them in half
gather some old dried charcoal and light
use homemade bellows to keep charcoal hot
hold over fire until golden brown
put some margarine on eggplants from red cross package
sprinkle with some rock salt and serve

Prison Camp Prunes

Get Dried Prunes from Red Cross package
gather some old dried charcoal and light
use homemade bellows to keep charcoal hot
put prunes and water in old margarine can
add some sugar and slices of lemon
boil to taste

Fish in a Ditch

After heavy rain - find one fish in a ditch
catch fish with bare hands
take back to prison camp
gather some old dried charcoal and light
use homemade bellows to keep charcoal hot
put fish on stick and hold over fire
cook to taste